WORCESTERSHIRE
COUNTY COUNCIL
CULTURAL SERVICES

DATE FOR RETURN

10   .06. MAR 14.
30   15. APR 14.
13   .18. JUN 14.
34 .07. AUG 14.

22. JUL 15.

23. MAR 16.

15. FEB .17.
22. AUG 18.

D0719079

700041058287

ON THE ROAD

Also by Richard Hammond

What Not to Drive
On the Edge
As You Do
Or Is That Just Me?

ON THE ROAD

Growing Up in Eight Journeys – My Early Years

RICHARD HAMMOND

Weidenfeld & Nicolson
LONDON

First published in Great Britain in 2013
by Weidenfeld & Nicolson

10 9 8 7 6 5 4 3 2 1

© Richard Hammond 2013

All rights reserved. No part of this publication may be
reproduced, stored in a retrieval system, or transmitted, in
any form or by any means, electronic, mechanical, photocopying,
recording or otherwise, without the prior permission of both
the copyright owner and the above publisher.

The right of Richard Hammond to be identified as the
author of this work has been asserted in accordance with
the Copyright, Designs and Patents Act 1988.

A CIP catalogue record for this book
is available from the British Library.

ISBN-978 02978 6943 6

TPB-978 02978 6944 3

Typeset by Input Data Services Ltd, Bridgwater, Somerset

Printed in Great Britain by Clays Ltd, St Ives plc

Weidenfeld & Nicolson

The Orion Publishing Group Ltd
Orion House
5 Upper Saint Martin's Lane
London, WC2H 9EA
www.orionbooks.co.uk

The Orion Publishing Group's policy is to use papers that are
natural, renewable and recyclable products and made from wood grown
in sustainable forests. The logging and manufacturing processes are expected
to conform to the environmental regulations of the country of origin.

To Mum and Dad for putting up with me on the bigger journey covered by this book and to my brothers Nicholas and Andrew who shared some of it. And to Mindy, my wife, for accepting the tattered remnants into her life. And to Izzy and Willow, setting out on their own roads.

CONTENTS

ACKNOWLEDGEMENTS

I should acknowledge people here because it took many of them to make writing this book possible. Mum, Dad, Nick and Andy, of course. And Mindy because, well, you always acknowledge your wife in this bit. Oh, and my agent, Luigi and publisher, Alan. Smashing chaps, thank you. But mostly, recognition should go to me for writing the bloody thing. It took ages, I mean AGES.

PROLOGUE

I want to explain myself before you read this book. Well, maybe that's what this book is about: explaining how I became the grown-up (ish) me. The journeys I'm talking about here are not big, heroic ones; there are no glaciers crossed, deserts trudged through or menacing jungle-passes conquered. All that came later for me. First I had to grow up. We all do. In this book I cycle to school aged eleven, or walk to work on a potato farm at fourteen or drive my first car home from Harrogate. In each instance, the journey represents another step on the longer journey towards adulthood from childhood. I think we've all made these journeys in the same bigger journey. These are the journeys where the travelling was not an end in itself, and even the actual end, when it comes down to it, was pretty inconsequential. And that's the point of the book. If you're riding a bicycle to the dentist across town then you're hardly likely to be too distracted by the scenery or the trials and tribulations of the journey. So what will be turning over in your mind as you go?

The journeys don't form us; we are forming as we travel.

And recounting those travels offers an insight into who we were at each stage along the way from child to adult. Writing about them has felt like sneaking up on myself, catching my younger mind relaxed and un-self-conscious. And I've been able to mine it for what was really turning round in there at each stage through my childhood and into adulthood. I'd forgotten the magical, riotous grip of a comic until I let myself be transported back thirty-five years to an endless drive in the family car to a holiday in Weston-super-Mare. I'd forgotten how important the close texture of a car seat can be, or the complex messages sent out by a young boy's choice of bicycle. I'd forgotten the teenage passions and anger that rejoiced in the piercing yell of my first motorcycle and pressed me to drive my first car on the road from Harrogate to Ripon just as crazily, selfishly and dangerously as the young lunatics I shout at today, as a middle-aged man.

You will have your own journeys, those moments when you can sneak up on your own past self and pry into your own head to see what was going on. Try it.

SOLIHULL TO WESTON-SUPER-MARE, 1978

The long, long drive to the seaside. I was eight, the car was ancient and the journey would take forever and ever.

Rain-streaked windows, the smell of sour milk, dreams of comic-strip heroes and adventures in the dunes. Are we there yet?

NOTHING will ever take so long . . .

It's a special, crushing, desperate kind of agony. And it feels like it will never end as the journey goes on and on and on and on and on. And there is no sense of it being a journey, with a beginning a middle and an end; a child's mind knows just an endless middle that starts as soon as the family car backs out of the drive. The distant end of the journey is a goal as unimaginable and unreachable as adulthood.

'We're off,' Dad would shout when we set off and briefly, for an infinitesimally short snap of firework time, we would be overjoyed, my brothers and I. We were off; the adventure was beginning. Our car was a magical spaceship, a Tardis that would transport us from our familiar, schoolday, Sunday-best Solihull with its parades of shops and cul-de-sacs and gates and over-under garage doors and the corner plots and cherry trees and white-flecked tarmac drives and all the infinite and subtle, grudging cues of suburban status and take us to the sparkling

3

excitement of the seaside with promises of exotic foods, beaches, buckets, spades, waves, piers and carnival parades of brightly coloured painted-metal posts-and-chains running along the sand-strewn promenades overlooking the wide stretches of beach. Hidden among the stiff, waving grasses of the rolling dunes armies lay in wait, ready to leap out to ambush us and many-eyed monsters hid beneath the sand knowing already in their dreadful, gnarled heads that we would hunt and dig and crush them.

My dad's parents lived in Weston-super-Mare and the journey there was a regular pilgrimage to see them. Regular but by no means often enough to please me and my two brothers or, I suspect, my nanna and grandpa who had sold up in their native Birmingham and moved there before I was born. They lived in a house near a corner opposite a church that we could see from the window of the room where we all three were put to bed, though seldom to sleep. On the ground floor of the house, behind a plain, hollow door, was Grandpa's serious surgery where he kept the chromed and dangerous tools of his work as a chiropodist. I don't know how he came to be a chiropodist. It's not something someone is born to. His career to that point had encompassed a spectacularly eclectic array of roles, from farm worker, truck driver, department-store food-buyer, through the terrors of bomb disposal work in the war and on to boarding house owner, chiropodist and cake-shop proprietor.

From a time barely scratched into my memory, they lived next to the cake shop that smelled of marzipan and icing. Sometimes Nanna would give us tiny decorative fruit made of marzipan, a delicacy of such rareness and value that eating them would have us squirming with a mixture of guilt and pleasure that would only become familiar again much later as we grew to be teenagers giving in to all the many guilty pleasures suddenly available to us then. Dad told me that Nanna once found a snake under the counter in the cake shop and had to carry on serving customers and pretending that nothing was wrong while calling Grandpa out of the side of her mouth to come and deal with it. That was the sort of thing that happened to Nanna and Grandpa, and one of the reasons we loved to visit them.

In the happy living room of the house with the chiropodist's surgery they had an ashtray on a tall, corkscrewed wooden stand and they would let us sit on the sofa and use it as a steering wheel in an imaginary car. I looked forward to the ashtray steering wheel as much as I looked forward to the early morning walks with Dad and Grandpa and my brothers along sand-scuffed streets past the quietest houses we could imagine to the paper shop that smelled of bread and sweets and glittered with bright, plastic seaside temptations that we looked at longingly but knew not to nag Dad to buy because he hated – and still hates – materialism. A child whining at their parent for a toy in a gift

5

shop was a sight so disgusting it could send our whole clan scurrying out to the street, full of sadness and shame for ever having walked in.

Grandpa's car had the best-sounding indicator in the world. It was, I think, an Austin Avenger, and it made the most delicate and musical yet important noise, 'bink-a-bink-a-bink-a', as he tilted the lever to navigate us round the busy seaside town. Many years later, when age had robbed his warm and gentle nature of some of its reactions and instincts, he was obliged to hand in his driving licence; while my dad wrestled with what he knew was a terrible and undignified loss for his own father, I mourned the loss of the familiar 'bink-a-bink-a-bink' in Grandpa's Avenger as we turned out past the church and set off for Bristol or the tiny Monk's Rest café that sat on top of a hill so steep that his car or any other car in the world, even a Ferrari or a Rolls-Royce or a Cadillac from the TV would struggle to make the ascent.

★ ★ ★

The transportation to my grandparents and this other world by the sea was not instant. Before we reached the end of our road the grey realisation would sink in and dominate our every childish thought. It was miles. And miles. And miles. A sort of panic rose up in me at the prospect. There would be arguments. That was a cold, dull fact. They hovered over the road ahead like storm clouds we must drive under. Dad would be forced to intervene and quell those arguments, to quash our boyish, riotous energies and stop them bursting out of the car in a multi-coloured shower of sparks. Having pushed Dad to the point of no return, we would sit quietly for a while, each lost in his own thoughts until the boredom could be contained no longer. It would leak out of us in tiny squeaks at first, building to a crescendo as one of us fought back verbally, stung into action at being squashed into the seat or by some whispered accusation levelled with laser-guided precision by a smirking sibling aiming for a nerve still raw from some earlier battle. We couldn't help it.

It must have been hell for our parents. On becoming a father I took a solemn vow that I would never allow my children's back seat riots to rattle me. I would remain calm and distant up front; a stoic, silent driver responsible only for the captaincy of his vehicle. And it worked ... Better still, perhaps as a result of being denied the buffer of my impotent fury to push against, my daughters don't fight in the car; they sit in companionable silence, lost in their books, or chat lightly, earnestly and intelligently. Or maybe it's because they are two girls and not three boys. I have never told my father this. It would, I suspect, make him grind his teeth a bit.

When we weren't arguing and fighting, we sang. The whole family did. We sang together and for hours on the long road to Weston, past the familiar landmarks and along the up-and-down bit where the carriageways of the infant M5 split — one direction elevated and affording travellers a lofty view across trees and fields, while the poor souls heading home to Birmingham skulked in the shadow of those whose holidays in the watery sun had yet to unfold.

I can remember the songs. My parents were folk singers — still are, in fact — and we worked up numbers from their repertoire as resident performers at the Bell and Pump folk club in the 1960s. We were familiar with 'Pretty Nancy of Yarmouth' and we sang of the 'long and fond letters' written to her by a sailor telling of his travels and adventures. We three boys knew the earthy urgency with which sportsmen were urged to arise, because 'the morning is clear and the larks are singing all in the air'. We sang and listened to our parents sing about workers in the huge gas plants at Birmingham or winding in ships' anchors or downing brown, foaming beer. And there were nonsense songs too:

Be kind to your web-footed friends
For that duck may be somebody's mother.
She lives in a swamp all alone,
where the weather is always down.

Now you may think that this is the end.
Well it is [*huge, dramatic pause*]

no it isn't, there's some more yet.
We'll start and we'll sing it again,
only this time a little bit lower.

And we would sing it again, a little bit lower each time, until our bright, childish voices dropped out of their register and could no longer reach down to join the impossibly deep, rich notes our dad would send reverberating through the car. No matter though, because we'd then substitute 'lower' with 'higher' on the last line until we were squeaking like mice. And then we'd repeat the song, finishing on the word 'quieter' or, best of all, 'louder' until we were roaring and laughing and shrieking loud enough to shake the car windows out of their frames and worry the people in the car next to us if they saw our red faces contorted as we screamed louder and louder and louder, the inevitable competition to be the loudest spreading like a brush fire through the three siblings cramped on to the vinyl back seat of the little grey Anglia.

When I first told my wife about these journeys and our singing, she cringed a little on my behalf. Embarrassed. But now my daughters sing in the car. They sing solo and together and my wife and I sing with them. Loudly. Pop songs. Rock songs. Nonsense songs. They have no video screens back there. They might listen to a song on their iPod briefly, but that only serves as a prompt for another number to share with us. Then we all join in and laugh

9

and sing and scream until passers-by and other drivers must stare and wonder about the four red faces straining for the top notes and grimacing when Daddy howls out of tune. I thank my parents for that. I really do.

★ ★ ★

Did cars have a stronger smell in those days or did our small noses, unclogged by age and experience and a million cigarettes and traffic jams work better? The Anglia smelled of burned petrol and smoke and vinyl and sour milk and hairspray. Windows have a particular smell if you sit with your head resting against one for long enough. Maybe it's the glass or some element within it. As the cat's eyes swooshed by and I dreamed of real cats lying in holes in the road, their eyes lighting the way, the familiar car smell washed over me until I didn't notice it and became absorbed into it.

The car lurched and squeaked over mysterious dark patches of road, like patches on a quilt, while the lampposts marched past in their millions. On night-time journeys I could let myself be hypnotised by the blazing, fiery archways of yellow light guiding us thousands of miles towards the sea. But today we travelled in the afternoon and nothing could alleviate the endless, grey grind of it as we wound our way on.

There were games as well as songs. Officially too old at nine for 'I Spy', I was still happy to let myself be drawn into it in the car, the game made excusable because there were adults involved. We competed to be first to spot a yellow car or a lorry or a phone box or a sheep. And we talked too. We talked about life, about places, about animals. We made up games where you would have to name something, an animal or town or whatever, beginning with each consecutive letter of the alphabet. A was always Aardvark. And Z was always Zebra. If you got those letters there was no point saying it out loud but no point looking for alternative answers because we couldn't think of any. We talked about death too. Children are fascinated with the subject. On one lengthy discussion about the longest forms of death, started by us morbid, gruesome little boys in the back seat, I argued that life, when you thought about it, was the longest form of death. I think my parents were a bit shocked by that one. I thought it was great and made me sound awfully clever and deep.

★ ★ ★

I'm reporting from a different planet. The world of a small child on a long car journey is a whole different world to the one you and I live in now. The surface of the seat, worn shiny and stretched by age is important, its texture the subject of intense and close study. There are tiny dimples in this apparently smooth surface and only I have spotted them. Staring at it, I can imagine it is the landscape of the moon and I am a spaceman in his ship, cruising over it. Or I am a scientist and this thing that only I have seen is important and must be examined. But the study makes me feel sick. I hate the way the vinyl sticks to the backs of my legs. There are lines across it where the panels are joined and the ridges leave imprints on my legs. It is impossible to sit comfortably for long, even with my young limbs. I can feel the springs through the thin vinyl. The car bounces and sits restlessly on other, bigger springs, great rusty ones, slung just under where I sit. The axle grinds between them. There is machinery down there, important, heavy, dark, unseen machinery doing its job like the engine of a ship. I close my eyes and imagine it working: spinning and pumping and sweating with oil.

There's a hazy smell of sour milk. My brother spilled it once. Or threw it up. Whatever, the event is lost in forgotten family history, but the smell remains, familiar to us all and as physically present as another passenger in the car with us. We don't even mention it any more but we never, ever take milk in the car; it's become one of Dad's rules. I feel sick now and open my eyes. I once tried reading in the car. That didn't work. It made me feel really, really sick. Comics are better; you can look at the pictures and it doesn't make you feel sick, but I don't have a comic. I get *Whizzer and Chips* sometimes. For a while it used to be delivered on a Saturday along with the papers for Dad. I don't have one now. I wish I did. I'll try to imagine what Sid's snake, Slippy, would do to liven things up. I can imagine him hissing his way from the back seat to the front, popping up between Mum and Dad with his red tongue sticking out, a vivid 'V' as he hisses and surprises them. Mum's curly hair would stand up in the air, straight. I imagine Sweet Tooth sitting next to me, his baby eyes big and round and his huge front teeth covered in candy. I like the word 'candy', it's more grown up than 'sweets', the word that we use. I try drawing my own comics sometimes, but it's not easy. The characters never come out like I see them in my mind. I would try and draw some now, if I had a pencil and paper with me on the seat.

I try Different Positions to Get Comfortable. After a while, I find one, a Comfortable Position. But inevitably something happens; I sit up to look out of the window, or move to scratch an itch where my sock has ground into my ankle, and then I can't find it, my Comfortable Position.

The car drones on. I have a headache. It's grey and heavy. I hate headaches. You can't escape them; they get you right where you live. If it's an ache in your knee or your foot, you can try and push it away from you, but if it's in your head, then you're stuck in there with it, like being in a lift with a crocodile. The world outside is dull and no longer tempting. I can no longer imagine running, being free, seeing grass, hearing water, laughing. I don't want to whine to my parents; I must be grown up and responsible. I am the eldest brother.

13

Will it NEVER END? I fold up into the corner, squashing myself into the seat and jamming my head against the side of the car, below the hard, vibrating window. I study the ashtray in the door. There is a red piece of Lego in it: a square brick, three-by-two dimples on top. I wish I could play with Lego in the car. But you can't. The pieces get lost and whatever you are trying to make gets broken and it makes you feel sick.

It is my turn to sit on the outside at the moment. That's why I can lean against the side of the car. Soon it will be my turn to migrate into the middle of the seat where there is nothing to lean against and you sit upright with your head lolling forwards, your chin not quite resting against your chest until your neck feels like it will never, ever be straight again. My brother is suffering that right now. He is pretending to be asleep. I don't think he is, but it would be unfair to wake him if he really is, so I stay quiet. I try to luxuriate in my corner, appreciate it while I have it. But I can't.

I look forward, past Dad's head in front of me, his hair thin and straight on the back of his neck, and I stare through the fly-streaked windscreen at the grey motorway advancing on us. Does he Get Bored when he's driving? Mum doesn't. She sits alongside him, looking out of the window and sometimes talking softly and smiling with him. They talk grown-up stuff. I can't think of anything to say. And I don't want to wake my brothers, who probably aren't asleep but might be.

We pass under a narrow, lopsided motorway bridge, taller than any other on the journey. It slants across the road, higher on one side than the other, with a rocky cliff face supporting the high side. I know the bridge, it is familiar. And it is hours and hours and hours from Weston. There is Nothing to Do and I am BORED.

We are living for one moment, all of us in this car. We are living for the moment when one of us announces that We Are There. The cry will go up: 'I Can See the Sea!' And we will all sit up and chatter and stretch and talk and plan and look at the familiar sights, welcome signs that the journey is over. It started as a competition, being the first to See the Sea, but nobody ever cares or remembers who is first to see it. We shout the words because it means We Are There and that's all that matters. Soon there will be squash in the bright plastic beakers with big white spots on them and Nanna's individual sponge cakes in tiny paper wrappers and Grandpa's white hair and big smile and seagulls shouting 'hi!' outside and the ashtray steering wheel and the long string light-pull hanging down over the big double bed that we use as a punchbag or to play a kind of tennis with until we are told to pipe down and go to sleep. But we don't, we whisper and play on until the noise rises once more and we are told we really have to be quiet. And then it is morning and the seagulls are calling outside the window with the chilly church and the paper shop. And all of that is as distant as the moon and it kind of upsets me

15

to think about it, makes a panic feeling rise in my chest and everything is worse and I wish I hadn't thought about it but it's too late now because I have and I squirm a bit and lose my Comfortable Position again.

I think I'm sleeping now. Or dozing. Maybe I'm dozing. But how do you know? And if you know, doesn't that mean that you can't be dozing? Now I know I'm not sleeping or dozing. I think I might be comfortable again now though. Except my left leg is starting to buzz with pins and needles. If you stay still for too long, they always come, the pins and needles. And sometimes their buzzing becomes unbearable. Why does that happen? Do grown-ups get pins and needles? I'll think about being grown up for a bit. How does it feel? Do they get bored? How do you know what you want to do as a grown-up? And what will I do? I'd like to do something exciting, something brave, something that will amaze people. Maybe I'll be an artist and draw comics. I'd love to do that. People would see my comics, see the characters I have created and admire them and laugh, and that would feel amazing. Maybe I can sleep after all. Maybe I'll be a spaceman. Somebody has to be, and it would be so exciting, up there ... away from everything ... king of the world ...

And a part of me, sometimes, is still there on the back seat, waiting to See the Sea.

Journey 2 Flying Solo

CYCLING TO SCHOOL, 1981

I had dreamed of a unicorn, but what I got was a donkey.
I learned to love it.
You have to love your first proper bicycle.
It's kind of a law.

The kid in the shed looks serious. He ducks below the worktop, head disappearing behind stacks of dusty flower pots, bags of Innes compost, trowels with dry, split wooden handles and faded plastic seed-trays full of failure and spiders. A flash of metallic red among the dull browns and greys: he is cleaning his bike. Seen through the clouded, cobwebbed windows, his pale face is creased into a frown and something in his brown eyes suggests that he is troubled by this task. In his hand is a white piece of cloth, probably from an old sheet, the edges fraying into cotton threads where it was cut. Down in the gloom behind the workbench, he runs the cloth slowly and tenderly over the length of the bike's diagonal down tube, taking care to navigate around the two gear levers that sit side by side against the sloping tube, before stopping to pay particular attention to something midway along it.

★ ★ ★

Yes, the kid is me. The shed is my dad's, behind our happy, semi-detached family home on the border between Shirley and Solihull, two suburbs of Birmingham. I am cleaning the bike in readiness for the ride to school. I know, that's unusual for an eleven-year-old kid: cleaning a bike before he rides it. We'll look at that later. More importantly, the bike, a red Peugeot Equipe, is wrong. It pains me to do this, but I must upset my parents here. You bought me the wrong bike.

There now, I've said it, it's out there and I don't think it reads too badly. I mean, this was thirty odd years ago. Three decades. I've met and married my wife, had two daughters, nearly died and become a famous TV presenter in that time. You've moved house five times, changed jobs, built businesses, watched all three of your sons traverse the treacherous cliffs of teenage years and make it into adulthood intact, sane and productive. You've gained three daughters-in-law and eight grandchildren and yes, won the odd grey hair since then. So, no hard feelings, surely?

Actually, it's impossible to imagine that there won't be hard feelings, because what I've just written there is, in the mind of the little boy in the shed at least, an issue of a gravity and significance on a par with my parents telling me that they had strangled the milkman.

Let us rejoin the kid in the shed with the bike. He is happy, in a detached, remote kind of way. Content in his work might be a better way of putting it. But there is indeed something lurking, something troubling behind those slightly too-big brown eyes in his young face. The bike is already clean yet he feels compelled to try to make it cleaner with a fresh rag, cut from an old sheet and saved for this very purpose.

I remember every millimetre of that bike. That in itself reveals how much machinery, motion, travel – all wrapped up in the early bloomings of a desire to break away from home – features in the mind of an eleven-year-old boy. So please excuse me if I revel a bit in the detail of it. It matters to young boys. Well, it certainly did to this one.

* * *

I pause with the rag, halting its sweep along the length of the down tube to inspect the two chrome bolts sitting midway along its upward-facing surface. Two and a half inches apart, the bolts feature Allen-key sockets in their heads. Part of the original fittings on the bicycle, their purpose is to accept a frame that would hold a drinking bottle, handy for a hard-working rider to rehydrate without stopping. Each bolt is secured by a silver washer with smartly milled edges clamped to the flat face of the threaded socket let into the frame to accept it. I scrutinise them. Sometimes the wax car-body polish I have borrowed – with permission – from the small supply of car-care products Dad kept on a shelf in the garage accumulates around the

21

base of the bolts and clings to the tiny gaps between the bolt-heads and the washers. It hasn't today.

Even though I have successfully removed all traces of the polish already, I run the corner of my brand-new cleaning rag over the bolts, just to be sure. I imagine the sheen of polish building up on the bike's frame, the lustre so deep you could fall into it, and I let my eyes wander over the machine. It's not so bad. Red is a good colour. My last bike had been red and I had loved it more than anything else the world could offer. And that bike had no gears at all and a weird, curved top tube, like an American cruiser bike. My Peugeot at least, has a proper frame. The truth of it is, I had dreaded this bike turning up. Now, as the most important thing in my life, I must force myself to learn to love it. It's a situation not unlike an arranged royal marriage in a kids' fairytale.

I had known I was getting a bike for my birthday. I didn't see how I could be getting anything else, so constantly had I mentioned wanting one over the preceding months. And with such a dogged, plodding, solemn determination. God but that must have been annoying. The bike I wanted was £110. That's not after adjusting for inflation and stuff. I mean the actual amount on the price sticker: £110. So what did that money represent thirty-two years ago?

The financial implications were meaningless to me. A price that huge attached to the bike of my dreams put it so far out of reach that it might as well have said a million pounds. It didn't stop me dreaming. It was kept on a rack at about eye height in the bicycle shop on the Stratford Road in Shirley. We visited that parade of shops a lot, Mum, my brothers and I; this was pretty much the main shopping drag and at some point in every week I would find myself face to chainring with my unicorn. A charcoal black frame stretched tautly between wheels of such razor-edged thinness I could imagine their dark, skinny tyres slicing grooves into the tarmac like pizza-cutters. The saddle stood tall and brutally narrow on its thin post, the tell-tale quick-release lever folded neatly away at the base of it, at the intersection of shiny chrome post and dark-painted frame.

The cable for the rear brake ran along the top tube, pinned straight between two metal lugs brazed on to the frame. The brittle black plastic cable shroud was barely visible against the deeply speckled, charcoal-black paint. It ran, together with its shorter, sister cable for the front brake, from the two elegant brake levers, each like a dull aluminium claw curving forward from the dropped handlebars' complex, sensuous profile. At the headset, where the handlebars joined the headstock and the down tube and crossbar met, the two cables divided to run back and down to the narrow, lightweight aluminium brake callipers, ready to clamp front or rear wheels in a death grip at the first touch of a finger on the waiting, sinister levers.

Each lever bore a capricious flick at their tip, extending forward in a manner that suggested they were unwilling to be confined into simply mirroring the handlebars' fuller, amply rounded lines. Eyes half-closed, I would gaze at them, fingers flexing as I imagined resting my hands against the levers' cold curves just above the forward flick at the tip, and then tightening, squeezing them, the metal warming as it pulled into the soft pillows of flesh between first and second knuckle on my index and middle fingers. They would be fearsome brakes, requiring skill and sensitivity in their deployment on a par with a racing driver squeezing the throttle or a marksman on a rooftop, finger on the trigger of a high-powered rifle with a deadly job to do and all the world counting on the result.

I cleared the thought, bringing fingertips into my palms in an impossible grip that would have snapped the levers clean off or catapulted me out of the saddle and into the waiting road had they really been in my hands.

Elsewhere across the bike's lean, savage geometry the details grew more intense, more obvious. It carried all the necessary cues of performance, placed with intricate precision across its brazenly athletic, lithe form. It had twelve gears. This meant a second chainring at the front, from which could be gained access to another entire range of gears using the same gear wheels at the back. My dad called this a 'double clanger'; a reference, I figured, to the metallic rattle of the chain itself being shifted between these two primary drives. But it was an ugly phrase, I thought, for such a significant and important device. Without it, a bicycle might be limited to five or six gears, using a derailleur at the rear to shift between cogs.

The term 'derailleur' hinted at something sensuous and intimate. Its job is to move the chain across from one gear wheel to the next, to 'derail' it in order to move it and change the gear ratio. The 'ratio' is the relationship between the chainring (the big cog at the front that you turn with the pedals) and the small cog at the back, the gear that drives the road wheel. If you want to go fast, a higher gear ratio means that every time your feet on the pedals turn the chain wheel at the front, they make the gear wheel at the back turn many, many more times. So you need a bigger chain wheel and a smaller gear wheel. But that's hard work. There's no such thing as a free lunch and it requires a lot of effort to turn the pedals even once. It's much easier, especially when you're pedalling uphill, if you have a lower ratio, with a smaller chain wheel and larger gear, because although every turn of the pedals results in fewer turns of the gear wheel, it requires much less effort. It's a trade-off, and it was a subject of fascination to me, with its principles and the sense of fairness of it, all wrapped up in logic.

And I loved the derailleur system. The idea that for the bicycle to perform at its best, for the many shining, lightweight parts to harmonise and maximise the rider's sweating input, it first had to be derailed, broken, disrupted in its most intimate and critical places, resonated and chimed unconsciously yet hotly in my little boy's mind. I am not reading too much into this business. It is true. Little girls have horses, this I know. Little boys have bicycles. Both matter very, very much to each in ways they don't really understand. And by the time they do understand, bicycles and horses probably don't matter to them any more.

My bike, the bike I visited and dreamed about in the shop on Stratford Road, had twelve gears, a feat it achieved by combining a double chainring – I refuse even now to use Dad's 'double clanger' – with a block of six gears at the rear wheel. The six, by switching to the second chainring at the front, is doubled to twelve. Cycling around suburbia on my old bike in the months leading up to my forthcoming eleventh birthday, I had become expert at spotting the tell-tale extra cog in the gear block at the rear wheel of bicycles I encountered on the streets. I could sneak up behind another bike, and in the second or two I had to spot the critical number before the rider sensed me looming behind on my tiny, fake racer with no gears at all and a funny frame, I knew whether that rear block carried five or six, and within a mere hundredth of a second more was able to confirm whether it bore one or two chainrings at the crank and from this extrapolate: five, ten or twelve.

A disturbingly large number of twelve-speed bikes

were appearing locally. This, it seemed was fast becoming the norm. My bicycle had none. I wanted, needed, gears and I needed twelve. My dream bicycle, the one in the shop, had twelve. It had quick-release hubs too, the wheels held in place by skewers that, at the push of a lever which reluctantly heaved over on its eccentric cam to loosen the clamps, allowed the rider to drop the wheel out of the forks as easily as he might take a plate from the drying rack by the sink at home. This was only necessary, of course, for the dedicated, hardcore racer like me. I savoured the word 'skewer'. It sounded right: Serious and specialised; lightweight and purposeful as a throwing knife.

★ ★ ★

Back to the boy in the shed behind the house in suburban Solihull. My birthday had come and gone. I hadn't fitted a bottle to my red Peugeot and those chromed bolts on the down tube stood proud, unfettered by the necessary aluminium frame housing a brightly coloured plastic bottle from which Tour de France heroes, exhausted by their efforts, would suck water. I wanted to keep the bike simple, stripped back. I relished the thought of anything free of unnecessary frivolities, as sleek and focused as a needle. If I didn't drink water, my bicycle didn't need to be burdened with a bottle. So I wouldn't drink water. Simple. It didn't have lights either. My previous bike had laboured under

27

the extra load of dynamo lights, the tiny wheel on the dynamo slamming across to the wheel rim at the push of a button, where it leaned heavily to be turned by the wheel, sapping the precious energy that my pumping legs were busily pouring into the bike to create motion, not light. Battery-powered lights were too expensive. And heavy.

I had found, in a sale tray at Halfords, 'quick-release' wheel nuts. These were not the quick-release skewers fitted to the special hubs on some bicycles, like the charcoal-black beauty of my dreams on the Stratford Road, but sort of like giant wing-nuts; standard wheel nuts really, but with the addition of huge, chromed wings to enable the user to tighten them with finger and thumb rather than reaching for a spanner. These then, were indeed 'quick release': I could fasten and unfasten them in seconds without recourse to the rounded-off box spanner I kept in the shed. I had only once found them worked loose, after my young fingers and thumbs had been unable to exert sufficient pressure to nip them up enough to keep them tight. They were heavy though. And the chrome had flaked off. They stood proud of the red forks on either side of the wheel, as if the ends of the spindle had frayed.

I scan the red frame. It's not a bad bike. It's a very good bike. Ten gears are plenty, especially considering my last bike had none. As my critical eyes catch the huge, 'quick-release' wheel nuts, I pause in my work, recalling the morning of my eleventh birthday. It had taken me a fraction of time too small to measure to realise that the bike waiting for me in the living room was not the charcoal-black, glistening beauty I had surveyed each week with lust and itchy fingers. The crashing disappointment was, in fact, primed and waiting, ready for deployment. It was no surprise when Dad called me in to my parents' room first thing, wished me Happy Birthday and said, 'Maybe you want to go downstairs, see if there's anything for you.' This was the moment I had been anticipating for the best part of the year since my previous birthday. In the meantime I had started at senior school, which was further from home than my junior school. I couldn't turn up on my old bike at my new school, with its fleets of bigger boys and its clock tower and playing fields with rugby posts and pavilions that smelled of summer and the scary, echoing refectory where sixth formers swaggered in stripy blazers, looking like they might just spark up a cigar after lunch and swill brandy with the masters. Dad's instructions to 'go downstairs and see if there was anything for me', confirmed it: my birthday present was the bike. Finally the moment had come when I could confess to my skipping heart that my old bike was too small.

My old bike, I told myself as I struggled to control my pace, resisting the temptation to hurtle down the stairs, was tiny. Minuscule. It looked as if it was made for a circus. I had loved it right up to this precise moment though; defended it with the ferocity of a mother guarding a cub.

When other kids turned up on bigger bikes with thinner wheels and gears, I pointed out the advantages of being smaller, lower, tucked under the wind that hit them full-on as they perched high on their huge bicycles with frames that were, I assured them, too big. I made a case for the purity of a bike with no gears being a lighter, less complex machine not likely to encourage the rider to waste valuable seconds fiddling around trying to work out which of his ten or even, for God's sake, twelve gears he was in. But I craved what they had; their tall, lean, stripped-down machines, glistening with a few critical pieces of menacing machinery, sparkling against the frame like rare diamonds in a coal face. Brake callipers and levers were matched pairs, rat-trap pedals and toe clips ready to grab the riders' feet as eagerly as a dog catching a ball and be powered round and round and round, sending the charge along the singing chain to the rear wheel where the derailleur assembly curled and coiled, ready to push the rushing, oil-slick chain-links across the teeth and on to the next cog in a seamless, urgent surge.

I couldn't park my tiny Puch next to their Peugeots and Raleighs and Dawes. I was, as I still am, quite small and didn't need to leave a visual and permanent calling card at the bike sheds to remind the threatening thugs in the years above that this guy Hammond, the one with the tiny bike, was a natural-born, made-for-it victim, smaller than you and back for business at his clown's bicycle later today. I sure as hell wasn't about to go sneaking about the place apologising either. I wanted a bike that put me on an even footing and then we'd see how things shook down. And the charcoal-black, twelve-speed Peugeot resting so lightly on its rack in the shop on Stratford Road that it looked like it could fly away if it weren't for the weighty price tag keeping it earthbound, would do it.

Alongside it in the shop I had seen another Peugeot. A red one. Simpler, with a lesser brake set, only ten gears, no quick-release hubs or toe clips, and an ugly black plastic chainring guard giving away its humbler intentions as a shopping and school bike rather than a demonic racer. It was £10 cheaper than the black one. Not an amount that I thought fully took into account the lower quality parts. But what did I care? I was getting the black one. And when, on my birthday, I pushed the door open to the living room, parents waiting upstairs to hear the gasps of delight their expensive gift would produce, I knew at the first flash of red that my dream had somehow got corrupted in the machine that turns dreams into reality and come out all wrong.

I put a brave face on it. Kids can sometimes. But as I pedalled away from the house and up our street on my inaugural ride, while my parents watched with smiling faces as I grew smaller, I thought of my black beauty with its twelve gears, its quick-release hubs, its toe clips and its wheels so thin they looked like they were made of paper.

31

As my trousers brushed against the thick black chainring guard on the expensive, brand-new but totally wrong gift under me, my heart broke. I know, it's far from the attitude of some child hero in a book, but there it is. A first taste of disappointment and joy and gratitude and guilt mixed. And a useful one.

So I set to work on it. There's a lot a boy can do to improve a bicycle armed only with a box spanner and whatever bits and pieces he can scavenge from his dad's garage. The plastic chainring guard went straight away. Just four bolts secured it and were quickly dispatched to reveal underneath a more purposeful, plain aluminium cog with teeth that could easily ensnare and ruin a rider's trousers if he weren't careful and skilled enough to avoid it: much more like it already. The reflectors secured to the brake callipers went; just a couple of bolts holding each of them on. The short mudguards were next to go; the thin metal flanges securing them to the same calliper mounts as the reflectors. Again, much more serious-looking now.

As I learned to accept this bike as my own, I made further cosmetic improvements. To protect the brilliant red paint from chips and scratches, I carefully applied electrical tape, borrowed from my dad's garage, to the underside of the bottom bracket and the chain stays where it was vulnerable to small stones thrown up by the wheels. Soaked by the rain, the tape turned into a muddy, matted mess and fell off, but it at least represented a step in the right direction; it meant I was falling in love with the machine. As I knew I must.

And now, in the shed, it was spotless and ready to ride to school.

★ ★ ★

I open the creaking door and wheel it out into the cold, clear morning and on to the uneven patio slabs behind the house before leaning it against the wooden fence leading to the walk-through to the front. I pull on my canvas rucksack, the thin straps slightly too tight to slip easily over the arms of my blazer, but I wrestle my way into it and tug the blazer straight. I tuck my tie between the third and fourth buttons on my shirt. Few things are more ridiculous to my eyes than a boy riding with his school tie flailing in the wind behind him like a streamer. My burgundy school cap is already stuffed into the rucksack. It would be impossible to hit the sort of speeds I intend hitting today and keep a cap on your head. I'll stop, wrestle off the rucksack and put on the cap before I make the last few turns to the school gates. For the rest of the trip, I'll risk being spotted by a master on his way in and the inevitable trouble that my bare head would stir.

Pushing the bike through the gap between our garage and our neighbour's house, I savour the tick-tick-tick

33

of the freewheel and imagine the tiny beak of the pawl inside, pecking at the sloping faces of the teeth on the inside of the chain wheel block as the wheel rolls innocently past. But I know that angled, fierce little pawl will bite back as soon as I start pedalling. My efforts will drive the chain wheel forward so that the flat, vertical faces on the teeth inside the chain wheel block will push against the suddenly stubborn pawl, turning the hub to drive the back wheel, thus translating my energy, my breakfast, into motion. It's like a magic trick and I look forward to performing it this morning.

I wheel it past the cherry tree that always blossoms on Mum's birthday and then on to the slope of the pavement where it meets the road at the end of our short drive. Steadying the machine, I ease my weight on to my left foot, ready to lift my right leg over the saddle. It is set at precisely the right height. When onboard, my leg will be fractionally off straight as the pedal hits the bottom of its cycle and my other leg powers the opposite pedal forward. I hoist myself up and over, school trousers snagging as my leg strains to clear the black, plastic saddle and I stand away from the crossbar, the saddle waiting behind me now. This seat-height set-up is the optimum for performance and efficiency on the move but makes for an ugly spectacle at the mounting stage. Rising high on to the toes of my left foot, I bend my right leg to flip the pedal round with the tip of my shoe and catch the metal toe clip as it rotates on its spindle then slot my foot home. The clips play hell with the polish on my black school shoes but they mean everything to me and I will risk disapproving looks and harsh words from the masters to protect these significant symbols of performance. The bike had no clips when I got it and adding them had been the single biggest expenditure of my life so far. Every penny of saved pocket money, birthday and paper-round cash had gone into them. But they were worth it.

Balance is essential now. My right foot is trapped in the toe clip and I'm standing with all my weight on the toes of my left foot. The chain lies across the third gear ratio at the rear and the inner, smaller ratio at the front. Third low: perfect for setting off, and offering a fractionally reduced risk of smearing oil on my school trousers, with the chain resting on the inner chain ring. Although that won't stop me stepping it on to the outer ring later, where it will almost certainly drag its oily length along my trouser leg and leave a tell-tale mark. I brace against the handlebars, push my weight down on to my right foot, turning the pedal and moving forward as I lift my left leg up and flip the pedal dextrously, feeling a familiar momentary surge of relief as my left foot finds the pedal flat and pushes into the waiting toe clip. And now I move off and into my realm, my world of rushing air, pumping legs, ragged breaths torn away by the wind, my neck straining forward over tensed arms as I hunch over the bars and pedal. This is where I want to be and where I am happiest. Moving. Rushing. In control. Just cycling to school.

★ ★ ★

Moving away now, I remember the mantra from my cycling proficiency test: Look over the right shoulder, make sure there isn't a car coming. There isn't and I can move off. Pushing hard, standing on the pedals, using my weight to turn them. Third gear in low ratio was a good start, but I'm going to need to change up soon. I love changing up. It reminds me of when I used to sit in the back seat of the car, in the middle bit where you can see between the front seats and watch the road ahead and see what Dad does to drive the car. He pushes down with his left leg on the clutch pedal, this disconnects the engine from the wheels of the car, then, with his foot still down, he moves the gear lever to change. I don't have a clutch on my bike, but I do need to ease off the pressure as I change. It's kind of like having a clutch and I do it consciously, keeping the chain wheel turning so that the chain moves across the gears, but not pushing down on the pedals too hard. That would grind the chain into the gear wheels and strain the cables running from the gear levers down to the derailleur, stretching them. The chain is well oiled, I check it every day and it makes a sort of slick, dulled metal noise as it glides across. That's the sign of a well-maintained bike.

It's cold today, but not so cold that the air freezes in my lungs; sometimes it's like breathing in ice cream and it really starts to hurt. Today it's fresh, but not painful. I hope I don't get chapped lips; I hate arriving at school with bright-red lips. It makes me look like a girl. There are no girls in my school, it's a boys' school. We talk about girls a lot though; some of the guys tell me stuff about what they do at weekends and in parks with girls. I don't really believe them but I don't tell them that. I pretend to believe and be impressed, just in case it's true.

I've changed into fourth now and I'm ready to go for fifth. That's Darren's house on the left, the one where the road bends round to the right at the top of the big hill. Darren loves football and whenever I think of him I think of those luminous sweatbands they wear on their wrists. My brother's got some, but I haven't. I don't play football really, never have. Ours is a rugby school and I have to play rugby.

Fifth gear. That feels great but it's time to go down the big hill soon and then I'll need to use the other gear lever and shift ratio on the chain wheel. The chain will move out to the bigger chain wheel, many times bigger than the smallest cog at the back, which means its much higher geared. For every time I turn the chain wheel with the pedals at the front, the little tiny cog at the back will have to whizz round about twenty times. It's much harder, but that's the beauty of it, the trade-off, the deal. That's how gearing works. And I'll use the downhill stretch to make it easier to pedal and pick up speed. When I hit the bottom of the hill I'll be doing about thirty miles an hour and will have to be ready for the sharp turn to the left, hanging on to the bars and leaning the bike so it's nearly horizontal. I got it wrong once, on a borrowed bike. When I knew I couldn't make the corner because I was going too fast and it was too tight and there was gravel all over it, I tried to stop but the bike was already leaning over too far and when I grabbed the brakes it skidded and I fell off. I ruined my left shoe and grazed my elbows. I didn't cry. I only say that to make it sound like I would never really cry and I'm just being funny pretending like I actually would. But I nearly did. I think it was the shock.

Football is horrible. Everyone just shouts and pretends to be people I've never heard of. I prefer rugby; it's more proper, posher. Rugby shirts are made of thick, warm material, not that nasty shiny stuff they use on football shirts. I've never had a football shirt. Or shin pads. I'd like some, but I'd hate to play football. I'm not really that good at rugby because the other boys are all bigger than me and that makes me angry. Sometimes I lose my temper when they tackle me hard just to be funny, and there's a fight. Once, I ran at a kid three times my size and he just picked me up as I butted my head into his stomach and threw me backward over his shoulder. I landed on my back and couldn't move or breathe. The air just wouldn't go in and out of my mouth. Everyone was gathered around me, lying there, but my chest wouldn't work. I couldn't get any air in and I started to faint. Everything went a bit blurry and misty and I put my head to the side so my cheek felt the cold grass and I could see the hedges at the edge of the school field, grey in the mist with the wire fences rising out of the top of them and the grass as pale as a sheet. I thought I was dying. I didn't feel panic any more, just very, very sad. And then my lungs worked again suddenly and I sucked in huge gasps of air, all shaky and noisy like I was having a giant asthma attack, which I don't have even though both my brothers and my dad do. I felt a bit daft to be honest. The breaths were huge, sobbing things, like I was crying. Which I wasn't. The games master told me I'd been winded and that's why I couldn't breathe. My solar plexus had gone into spasm and maybe if I really was fainting that's when it relaxed and I could breathe again. All the other boys thought I'd broken my back and were dead impressed. I'd thought I'd broken my back too and was absolutely terrified. But I didn't tell them that.

This is the hill now. See, it's huge. Sometimes, when there's a car heading up it towards you and another coming from behind, you feel like there isn't going to be room at the bottom to make the big sweeping turn to the left, but then you're in it and there isn't time to think about it. The

39

air's making a huge noise as it rushes past my ears. There's no need to stand on the pedals going downhill, I can sit on the saddle and tuck my arms in, ducking down to keep low. It's more aerodynamic this way, like skiers on the TV. There's a massive road junction after the bend at the bottom. I have to pull hard on the brakes as soon as the bike is upright after the corner.

And here it comes. I'm in the corner. When I stop pedalling like this, I can hear the freewheel clicking. I love that noise. Pedals still. Keep the left pedal up so that it doesn't dig into the tarmac and tip me off. I did that once. God it hurt. The pedal must be just about on the floor now, even though it's up and the right one is down. Don't touch the kerb though, that'll be an accident for sure. I did that once too. You get the wheels both stuck against the kerb and you can't turn away because there isn't room for the front wheel to turn and you can't go up the kerb because it's too close and steep, and you know you're going to fall off and you've just got to wait for it to happen. It's awful. I'm through the corner, there's this little straight bit with the posh houses on the right and the triangle of green behind me, and up ahead is the junction. This is a busy road. Have to be really careful here. Too many cars coming now, I'll have to wait.

That's the Prospect Lane shops, over there, to the right, on the far side of the road. There's a butcher's and some other shops, and the newsagent where I do my paper round every Saturday and Sunday. I hate Sundays – all those huge papers. I have to make two or even three trips because they're too big for my bag and it weighs a ton and the strap pulls thin and feels like it's going to cut through my shoulder. And why do some people insist on ordering the *Sunday Times* with a million sections in it when all they've got is one of these tiny vertical letter-boxes with a massive spring in it so you can hardly push it open? Guaranteed, when you do finally push it open, your fingers go inside as you push the paper through and then it springs back and locks on to your knuckles and you can't get your fingers out again without leaving half your skin stuck to the flap. It's like your hand is being eaten by a shark with those teeth that point backwards to stop fish escaping from their mouth once they've caught them.

I got so sick of it once that I took every page out of every section, rolled them up lengthways and posted each one through the flap, holding it open with my other hand or it would have closed and shredded the pages. When I finished, the pile of paper in their hall reached up so far I could see the dark shape of it through the frosted glass of the front door. I bet they were furious. I kept thinking I'd be in loads of trouble back at the shop, but I never heard a thing about it.

Right, no cars, I'm going to cross straight over and go across the green. It's one of those big greens where there's loads of grass and some trees but no park, no playground.

The trees are all small; young, I suppose. It's ever so quiet. It's weird, but I really like it. There's a snaky path you're not supposed to ride your bike along but I do because there's never anyone here this time of the morning anyway. It connects up with another road at the other side that brings you out in front of the school I went to before, Sharmans Cross Junior. I'll be turning left there to head down another hill, nothing like as big as the one on our road and then turn right towards Solihull town centre. My new school is the other side of town and I have to cycle right through to get there. I was nervous the first time I did it, but now I enjoy the ride. It makes me feel grown up. I prefer being here though, on the green.

I love it on the green when it's been snowing. It hasn't snowed today, obviously, but I love it when it has. Especially on paper-round days when nobody's walked on it yet and it's just a sea of new white snow. I almost don't like to make tracks across it and spoil it. But I do. I think about Scott of the Antarctic then. I'd love to be a polar explorer. This cycling is good training. I sometimes wonder if I can stand the cold better than most people, if maybe I've got, like, special blood or skin or something and I am kind of destined to be an explorer. I loved reading about Scott and his trip to the Pole. He died in his tent, not far from the Pole itself. The saddest thing was that he left a letter for his wife, telling her how brave the men had been and how they were all running out of food. He knew he was going to die. And he wrote his wife a letter. What would you say? How would you even write a letter like that? Wouldn't you spend all your energy trying to make a machine out of wood that could save you, or hunting a polar bear to eat? Not that they have polar bears at the South Pole. I don't think they do.

Anyway, the air is cold today, but more a damp sort of cold, the kind that makes your hands burn but doesn't make breathing hurt. Funny that; your hands burn with cold. But they do. It's a similar feeling, burning and freezing. They talk about freeze-burns, in fact. If you grab hold of something metal at the North Pole with your bare hands, the skin freezes to it and when you take your hand away, your skin stays on the metal. That's a cold burn and it's really, really painful. I read a lot about frostbite too. That really hurts and your fingers go black and fall off. I once thought I'd got frostbite when I'd been playing in the snow making snowballs for hours and hours with no gloves on and my hand felt like it was on fire when I went inside. Dad told me it was chilblains but they sound crap, like something an old person gets. I thought mine was frostbite. But nothing turned black and fell off, so it wasn't. Probably for the best.

I'm going to really go for it now, pedal until my legs are on fire and my lungs burst and my hands burn with cold and I'm not going to get chapped lips and I'm not going to let my tie get out of my shirt and make me look stupid and when I get to school it's going to be a great day, I'll be really funny in class, make a teacher laugh with a clever, witty line and have a fight without having to actually fight and I'll draw an amazing picture of a car in Art, and Maths will be cancelled and so will Games because of rain and then I'll go home again. And I doubt you can keep up. So come on, let's go ...

WALKING TO WORK AND A FIGHT, 1984

I wasn't just walking to work. I was making my way through the dangerous stretch of no-man's-land between childhood and adulthood. With a mind full of dreams, lusts, fears, violence and poetry.

It's tricky being fourteen, but it can be fun too. Walking felt best then; time to think and maybe do some growing up. Or not.

I wanted to be a tramp. Not a desperate, needle-pocked, live-in-a-skip type of tramp, obviously, but a proper tramp. A lonely wanderer, a strider of sun-mottled lanes, guardian of the hedgerows, bearded, wise, as old as the sun and forever young as the freshest spring buds. That sort of a tramp, the sort of a tramp that lingers in the leafy byways and grassy roadsides of a fourteen-year-old boy's wandering, yearning mind.

The family had left Birmingham suburbia for rural North Yorkshire just a few months earlier. We weren't yet living in a whitewashed, thatched cottage with a rose-framed, Hobbity doorway, but the small, suburban semi we rented was just temporary. We would soon move into our own home. This, I knew, would be exactly the sun-splashed, rain-lashed escape from the looming threat of adulthood that I needed.

I walked a lot. Not merely because I couldn't drive, but because I loved the process, the simple plodding progression across a landscape achieved by my own uncomplicated but undaunted efforts. I loved the measures, the meter of it; the rate at which things arrived in front or alongside me, to be examined, considered and then allowed to drift into the past behind me.

I had always walked. I loved my bicycle, the escape, the speed, the glamour of it, but I loved the pared-down simplicity of walking. Me making progress in the world in the simplest way I could. No room for bullshit; no amount of parental wealth, brainy confidence or unearned brawn could compensate if, when it came down to it, you failed to send the simple command to your legs to move you ahead. Besides, walking gave me time to think.

I was walking today to a farm where my mate Benny and I had bagged ourselves a few days' potato-picking. It wasn't well paid and it would be tough work. Apparently we would have to spend hours in the fields, bending to pick the potatoes from the cold earth and put them in a basket. What happened after that, none of our friends had been quite clear on, but I figured I would find out soon enough when I got to the farm.

The walk there was across familiar ground. From our rented house on a small estate on the outskirts of Ripon I could pick up paths and lanes I used often either to run or to walk the dog – or to sneak off from the family for a quiet cigarette and a think. The lanes were rough, well worn and broken up and the tracks were muddy and pungent.

★ ★ ★

As I walk, I turn the day over in my mind. I have never been potato-picking, but there are two things about it that I love already: it is simple, manual labour, outdoors. And secondly, it takes place in autumn, my absolute favourite season. I suck in the misty air, smiling and narrowing my eyes with pleasure as the damp clings coldly to my throat and rolls through my chest. The sky is a milky, diffused white of the sort that leaves me feeling as though I am walking inside a light bulb. The mist is fine and thin, just enough to mute colours and make the gateposts and fence-rails and trees I pass stand out black against the pale fields. I shiver inside my jacket. It isn't thick enough to keep out the cold and damp on the walk there, but I know that once I get to work I will warm up and soon be steaming through the thin layers of nylon and polyester like a race-horse through its blanket. My boots are proper walking boots; leather, slick with dubbin. I am planning to meet up with Benny at the farm, which means I have the pleas-ure of walking there alone – the best way to walk.

The lane I am following drops slightly to a ford beside a lonely house. Here I leave the broken tarmac and take to a path across the fields. The countryside is broad and largely flat here, bordering the rich farmland of the Vale of York. Walking across it this morning, I imagine Romans marching and rugged farmers working these very fields.

49

Crossing the ford, I try to imagine how cold the water bubbling around the dark, steely granite stones must be and stoop to dip in a finger and test it. It is freezing, but it feels as though the ends of my narrow fingers are burning. The stream makes a rich gurgling noise, strangely warm in contrast with the cracking cold as it burbles hollowly around and over the stones where it crosses the lane.

Today will be a good day. We will pass it outside in this slow-moving, majestic autumnal mist and earn money to spend later. I want a leather jacket. I'm hoping to have a motorcycle in a few years but I figure, if not the bike, I can at least have the jacket in the meantime and signal my intention. A new jacket would be well beyond my reach; I don't know how much such a thing would cost, but undoubtedly it would be way more than I could hope to raise. But some of the guys I know at school have older brothers who ride bikes, and maybe one of them will have a jacket to sell one day soon. Or maybe something will turn up in a jumble sale in the church along the road from our house. I picture myself walking these paths in a black leather jacket; the thick metal zips rattling and the leather creaking as my arms move. I imagine I'll feel like a character from *The Lord of the Rings*, dressed for mortal combat with any passing hordes of orcs or a Rider. My anorak is soaked from the mist now, damp like a tea towel after the ritual of the Sunday-lunch washing up.

Why can't I just do this forever? Walk on through the landscape, passing trees black in the mist and slick with water, crossing crystal-clear fords where streams rattle stones like bones in a cave. I long to be a tramp. There must be a brand of functioning, useful type of tramp. Could I accumulate knowledge and wisdom from the earth and the sky, somehow soaking it up the way my jacket is soaking up the mist, and then exude it usefully? Maybe if I were an artist. Maybe I could create things of such potency and vigour that they would contain and then transmit these natural energies I had absorbed from the world around me; a world that only us privileged tramps get to see as we wander, pitching our bodies and souls into the search for wisdom. The world will be my canvas, though I see myself not as the painter but the paintbrush. I think like this a lot, when I walk. The rhythm of my own steps quietens my conscious mind like a lullaby, leaving my broader subconscious to wander free, like the tramp of my dreams.

The morning feeds my senses only with what it chooses for me. Sounds are muffled and softened until only the ones the morning selects for me can filter through to my ears. A thin branch might creak or a bird make the softest squeak in a field hundreds of yards away, yet I'll hear it through the drapes of the mist as clearly as if it were on my shoulder. I can hear nothing of the city behind me now, only the select menu of sounds brought to me

51

one by one by the morning. And it chooses what I see too. There seems to be no constancy to the mist's hanging veils. I couldn't see the top of the small house by the ford as I passed it, but now, across the milky fields, I can see a solitary tree, black and feathered in the far distance against a low hedge reduced to a single stroke of muted green. It's dizzying because near and far are blurred, perspective is compressed and then stretched until I feel both tiny and huge in a landscape alternately intimate and vast.

Crossing the fields here takes me past a raised line of hawthorns, especially black and ancient this morning in the mist. Their grizzled heads resist the soft caresses of the mist as though it were a silk sheet dragged across a bed of nails. Thorns stand out black and sharp and streamlined as tiny missiles, each with a glistening bead of water hanging heavily from the tip of its pointed snout. I can smell the fields now, the grass and the manure, even the trees themselves, earthy and alive in the mist.

The grass here is cropped short by sheep; the remnants of it cling close to the ground, just a thin, stubborn green carpet resisting their nibblings. It rises up to the gnarled feet of the hawthorns where they stand on a ridge formed after countless centuries of tilling and toiling have raised the divisions between fields into a topographical feature as surely as the volcanoes and glaciers of our geography lessons scour and scrape and raise the earth. I loved learning about glaciers: vast and unstoppable, relentless as time, writing their stories into the earth over a span of years unimaginable to us with our organic limitations and daily obsessions.

A narrow gate at the end of the line of hawthorns signals a sudden descent of a few yards traversing gnarled tree roots and slick stones, pressed into the mud as steps: a far less lasting and impressive transformation of the landscape than the gradual scouring of the fields and setting of the ridges between them.

The woods are damp and dark; the mist here hangs grey between dripping boughs. The leaves of low-lying plants between the glistening tree trunks are dark green and primordial. I feel a brief moment of earthy lust shiver through me and wish I had a girlfriend to share it with amid the wet undergrowth and the glossy leaves. Our flesh would glow fantastically pale against the dark ground and we would catch and snag ourselves on the brambles and thorns, scraping and scratching, leaving marks that would, for a while, remind us of our primeval encounter ... I quash the thought; this isn't the time – it never is – and move on towards the waiting farm and the work.

The farm is big and dark. Massive buildings behind high walls of grey stone made black by the morning and the mist. In open-fronted barns lie tractors and machinery, glinting under the dust among the bails and sacks and barrels and tools. In the yard, a man in muddied green overalls with a John Deere logo on the breast is taking names from a gaggle of kids, mostly boys my age or a bit older, turning up for the work. Underfoot the ground is stony and slick and I stamp the mud from my woodland forage off my walking boots. I should have worn wellingtons; everyone else gathering nervously or confidently in the soft drizzle that's now started up is wearing them and I feel silly. My footwear is betraying my suburban past. Benny is there and he greets me with a broad smile. He's more confident than me – everyone is – and laughs and jokes with strangers while we wait.

★ ★ ★

The work turns out to be as backbreaking as promised. We line out across broad, brown fields following a tractor dragging an implement to uproot and loosen the potatoes from the earth. As it advances slowly, we walk behind it obediently. There's something medieval about the sight of this thin row of boys, working the dark fields behind our dragon master. Each of us has been equipped with a green plastic basket; as we rode the trailer down to the fields the farmer – terrifyingly tall, with hair as wild as his own crops in high summer – explained how we must stoop to pull the potatoes from the ground, shake loose the soil, then throw them into the basket until it is full. We then tote our haul to another machine behind another tractor and tip them in. There was more, but his words kept getting lost in the noise from the tractor and my mind was elsewhere. It had suddenly occurred to me that we were passing lines of electric fencing and the edges of the wooden trailer we were sitting on were metal. If I were to grasp the fence while keeping a hand in contact with the metal strip on the trailer, would everyone leap up in shock? I didn't have the nerve to see it through, but thought it might work. Then again, no; they wouldn't be earthed, so it wouldn't work. Anyway, I think the machine's supposed to shake the remaining soil from the potatoes, but it could just as easily polish them until they turn into precious stones for all I know. One thing's for sure: I daren't ask the question and compound my mummy's-boy-boots with a display of ignorance on the finer points of our manly labours.

I'm happy in the work though. It's everything I hoped it might be. The banter along the line is good and I even risk a few jeers and jokes with some of the smaller, younger boys. Some of them look like urchins from a film of a Dickens novel; hair shaved to a fuzz on their thin bony heads and their tough, rural bodies wrapped in jeans and jumpers and jackets of muted colours and natural, well-worn fibres. Feeling as suburban as a fake wishing well on a manicured lawn, I overcompensate, swearing until I forget the words I meant to put in between the swear words to give them meaning.

Benny is better at this than me. He's bigger and tougher

and funnier and has made friends with several of our fellow workers. At midday, we gather in the margin of a field for lunch. There are maybe fifteen of us. The farmer tells us we have half an hour to eat whatever we've brought and that we mustn't stray from this wet, grassy patch while he goes off for his 'scran'. The bigger boys perch around the sides of the trailer that brought us down to the fields. The tractor that hauled it has been unhitched and is parked a hundred yards away along the grassy margin. Benny and I lean against a crumbling stone wall and talk with two boys: one is long-haired, a heavy metal fan like Benny and me, but older and therefore free to demonstrate his allegiance with his long, pale locks, hanging lank in the damp.

He walks over to the trailer, ignoring the other boys laughing and chewing their lunch, and reaches in to pull out a leather jacket. As he walks back towards us he shrugs the jacket on, settling it on his shoulders before pulling a cigarette packet from the inside pocket. 'Fookin' cowd, 'n't it?' He grins out of the side of his mouth as he raises a tarnished bronze Zippo to the end of his cigarette. The other boy in our new sub-division of the pack is a skinhead. And not just because of his shaved hair. Plenty of other boys, some of them only twelve or thirteen, have similarly bony skulls under their woollen hats and flat caps. But theirs looks to be a parental choice, perhaps for the sake of convenience at bathtime or maybe to match an equally shorn father. Our friend has the shaven head but also the green bomber jacket, tight jeans and impossibly high Doc Martens to complete the look and make it clear that his head has been shaved because that's how he wants it to be and it would be best not to ask him about it.

He may be terrifying to look at, but he turns out to be really very nice to chat to. Quiet, soft-voiced and sincere, he talks earnestly about the countryside and the day, responding only to questions asked and not volunteering anything outside of our banter. Benny is typically loud and funny, challenging the heavy metal fan on lyrics from songs by Rainbow and Deep Purple, and laughing at jokes about girls and drinking. It's my job to sit close to them and chip in what I can, when I can and, as I see it, to make sure Benny doesn't go too far and provoke the heavy metal fan into anger. Not that there seems any danger of that; the guy is laughing and joking and lighting another cigarette halfway through an anecdote about going to see AC/DC with his friends.

The skinhead has wandered off a bit and is standing by a pile of old straw and fence posts. He bends to pick something up and sets off back to us. In his hands cowers a baby rabbit, looking scared and cold. Our crew agree that it's probably got myxomatosis and is pretty much dead already. But the skinhead turns away, his broad shoulders straining the damp material of his tattered bomber jacket as he shields his new charge. He walks back to the pile of rubbish and, with infinite care, lowers the rabbit into a secluded hole and sits alongside it on the wet ground. The heavy metal fan smiles and shrugs and resumes his conversation with Benny. I watch the skinhead.

Another group of boys, over by the trailer, are jostling and fighting in the soft drizzle, but it doesn't look serious, just fun. I'm glad not to be caught up in it though. Three of the bigger boys have wandered over to the tractor, where it stands like a lonely cow. It's a small tractor, clearly very old, maybe used specially and only for pulling the trailer with us kids down to the potato fields come harvest time. Its headlights, round and wide, stand proud of the rounded bonnet on stalks, giving it an innocent and questioning air. It is, I decide, a very nice-looking tractor.

As the others talk and fight and the skinhead watches the baby rabbit in its nest and hopes it won't die, I watch the boys by the tractor and hear it cough and chunter into life, the faithful old diesel settling into a practised, contented burble. It shudders across its entire frame as one of the three boys who are now crouching on it like demons tormenting some creature, jabs it into gear. It moves only a few feet and then stops, the boys hurriedly shutting it down and moving away from it. They have seen the farmer approaching, I know it. And turning to look down the field, I get confirmation. Striding towards us under the grey trees hanging over the wall is the matchstick-man figure of the farmer in his overalls. He's still some way off but I can hear his big wellingtons slapping against his calves as he strides not towards us but straight towards the tractor. He's seen the boys start it, he must have done. And certainly he will have heard them.

His grey hair is thick and leaps about on his head, alive, maybe fired up by the anger that is clearly raging through him. He's carrying a stick, but as he gets closer, he throws it away. I wonder if this is some unconscious measure to ensure he won't be responsible for the death of an adolescent boy. He gives one cry, a single syllable as he arrives at the now silent tractor. The boys who started it have had the sense to run away, but not to blend back in with the group. Instead they have stopped halfway and turned to stand transfixed, captivated by their doom bearing down on them. The farmer is magnificent now, towering above us, his size exaggerated by the uniform green of his dark overalls. The tractor, I realise, is parked on a slight mound at the edge of the field and the farmer stands alongside it, arms moving in frustration as he searches for words. I feel his eyes on us and I feel them sweep away and focus on the three miscreants now backing into the gaggle of boys.

There is a pause, a delay of some seconds as the farmer's fury bubbles and roils inside him. And then he simply explodes. He's beyond magnificent now – spectacular. He reaches behind the tractor's rudimentary controls, behind the bonnet and between the big back wheels, and pulls out a slender black object. It's a metal bar, sharpened into a double prong at one end. A crowbar, about two feet long. And as he rages about what the boys have done to his precious tractor, how they don't know how to drive it and could have wrecked it, he beats the syllables out on the tractor's bonnet, every blow ringing in the damp, autumn air as if he were a farrier striking his anvil. With every blow he carves another crease into the thin tin. His words have joined together, the syllables merging into one continuous roar.

Eventually, the farmer, his fury vented, turns and walks off, disgust radiating from every pore. The boys who drove the tractor have, not surprisingly, slunk into the crowd, but their sagging shoulders and open mouths give them away. It will be a while before their adolescent bravado can prop them up again. Back on its lonely mound, the tractor looks on with its wide, puzzled eyes, its brow now furrowed by the farmer's beating. The skinhead, still sitting in the wet grass by the pile of straw, turns quietly to look into his baby rabbit's nest, his own brow similarly furrowed.

As the afternoon wears on, I can feel the tension building. It's good work; good hard, manual labour, but it is tedious and dull and no amount of teenage joking and japery can relieve that monotony. Benny tries. As the afternoon darkens, under increasingly heavy skies, he hunkers down on the broad, dark brown expanse of dirt, away from the rest of us, and I can hear a soft muttering from where he is crouched. I look across at our new friends. They are both hard at work, lifting the potatoes and filling their baskets. I imagine that their fingers are like mine by now, sore and red. Slivers of the raw vegetable for which we are scrabbling in the ground have wedged under our nails. It's getting colder and the cold numbs some of the pain after a while, only to release it in bigger gobbets as the work warms my fingers briefly.

The heavy metal fan looks up at me and smiles and I nod towards Benny, a distant figure, hunched over the soil, stationary and alone. We can both hear him chuntering now and it's obvious that one of us is going to break first and go over to hear what he is saying. I stand, young legs unbowed even after a day's work in the cold and damp, and walk slowly across, hoping not to be spotted by the farmhand working the machinery. As I get closer I can make out the words and, unexpectedly, a tune, but I can't quite make sense of it. Benny is singing quietly, his face turned to the ground, but I can see that he is watching me out of the corner of his brown eyes, desperate to share the joke but determined not to spoil it. I walk closer still; the tune is familiar now, it's more of a chant than a song and the words slot into place. Quietly, happily, Benny is singing as he lifts the potatoes with numb, bloody hands

61

and places them in his basket: 'One potato, two potato, three potato, four ...' And I explode with laughter, the unexpected joy of it bursting the dam of tension that has built through the long, hard afternoon. Heavy Metal Fan and Skinhead immediately join me and Benny keeps up his chant long enough for them to share the joke before he too gives up and rolls on to his back in the mud and laughs until his tear-streaked eyes can't see us standing over him.

'You big daft twat!' Heavy Metal grins and pokes him gently in the side with a boot.

★ ★ ★

We are paid in cash and I pocket mine eagerly, resolving to start a collection in a jar at home so that I can eventually buy a leather jacket like Heavy Metal Fan's. He and Skinhead say goodbye to Benny and me; a handshake would feel too formal and is not yet an acceptable currency between me and my contemporaries. Then Benny and I walk off the farm. Our paths home follow the same route for a mile or two, so we walk together, reflecting on the day and recalling the farmer's awesome explosion and the way he took out his anger at the boys who nearly ruined his tractor by ruining his tractor. I feel another burst of the same joyous laughter we shared at Benny's joke in the field building up, but stop when I see that the path ahead is blocked.

We are walking along a narrow gulley, more of a broad ditch really, between two grassy banks. Ahead of us, astride a motley collection of bicycles, is a group of the boys we have spent the day working with. At the front are two of the three who briefly stole the tractor and in doing so, earned it its savage beating.

'Where you fuckin' going?' one asks. I cringe inwardly. Not because of the question but because it is directed at Benny. Like me, Benny is physical and, like me, he isn't scared of a fight. We have had a few at school, though never together and certainly not against one another; Benny is, I suspect, a lot tougher than me and I have worked hard to avoid a flare-up between us. Confronted by this kid and his mates in front of me, there's no way Benny is going to back down. I know it will be a matter of seconds before this turns sour.

Sure enough, the leader takes a step towards Benny and swings a wild haymaker at his head. Benny ducks it and springs up, ready to fight, but the rest of the gang rush forward and he disappears as four or five of them surround him, throwing increasingly vicious kicks and punches at his now prostrate body.

For a moment I'm frozen but aware that I need to galvanise myself into doing something. Benny's single shout of my name, muffled by flailing arms and legs, stirs me into action. I take a step towards the melee, but as I do I see that the rest of the gang are watching me with the cold, baleful eyes of wolves. It's obvious that I'm going to have to fight my way out of this one, just as Benny is doing, frantically now, behind me.

I am still wearing my canvas rucksack and decide that this will only hamper whatever I can do to beat off these guys long enough for Benny to get to his feet and help. I start to slip the narrow canvas straps off my shoulders, moving as slowly as a cornered suspect putting down a gun in a cop movie. With one strap now nestling in the crook of my left elbow, I start lowering the other one. I think about saying something that will calm the advancing lads, but I know that it's bound to come out wrong and I'll just sound scared or stupid. Instead, I concentrate on wriggling the strap of the rucksack down my right arm. It too now sits in the crook of my arm and I realise, too late, that both my arms are now pinned to my sides at the elbow. The advancing attackers, pretty much on me now anyway, also realise this and slacken their pace long enough to enjoy the scene, eyes widening with evident pleasure as they realise that this is going to be very easy indeed. And it is.

One throws a punch which half connects with my cheek. I turn my head away from it, riding the punch as best I can, shortened arms swinging from the elbow and making me look and feel like a tiny dinosaur in big trouble. If I could only stop everything for long enough to relax my arms behind me and slip out of the rucksack, I might be able to do something to hold them off, but I am under attack and relaxing my arms is not what's raging at the forefront of my mind. Another punches me in the stomach, the thing I dread most, but as I double over I twist away and manage to wrestle an arm free of my rucksack's treacherous embrace. Throwing the rucksack to the ground, I turn again, facing my attackers with left shoulder dipped and my eyes scanning for revenge.

And at that moment everything changes. I hear a shout from a short distance away, followed by another, both clearly delivered on the run. I can look up to see what and who it is because the boys attacking me, secure in their numbers, have done the same. And it is Heavy Metal Fan and Skinhead, running towards us. Heavy Metal's leather jacket glistens in the evening air and Skinhead's bomber jacket billows in the wind as they run at us, full tilt, as though they won't stop until they have run straight through. The team beating Benny stops now, heads turning to see our two champions advancing – because this is what they are: our champions. No one would stand in the face of such advancing fury and menace.

Sure enough, our attackers run. There's barely a shout between them as, like a herd of wildebeest spotting lions advancing on the grasslands, they turn and bolt. Skinhead and Heavy Metal reach us as Benny is getting to his feet. He's not hurt; it was a schoolboy beating, nothing more. I hope for a heroic bruise on my face, but will be disappointed when I get home to find none. Skinhead and

Heavy Metal laugh when they see that we are OK and ask us what it was about. We don't know. I secretly suspect that they took exception to Benny's happy, carefree, confident joking and his theatrical gag, singing as he put the potatoes in his basket.

Looking back at the battlefield, it's obvious just how scared our attackers were at the arrival of our rescuers: they have abandoned their bikes. Gaudy BMXs and racers lie stricken in the long grass like so many downed dragonflies. We all four run, laughing, back up to the farm and knock on the farmhouse door to explain in panting gasps to the farmer what happened, so if he finds a load of bicycles in his fields he won't be too puzzled about where they came from. He thanks us and slams the door. We say our goodbyes again, Skinhead, Heavy Metal, Benny and I, and this time head off on our separate ways without incident.

★ ★ ★

As I followed the lane through the dusk home I filed the day away in my tramp's memory store of experiences on the road, doing my best to suppress thoughts of the gang returning to find me alone and without my unpaid bodyguards. The knowledge that the pocket of my anorak held eight pounds to start my leather jacket fund helped dispel all other worries.

Rumour had it that the farmer, in a rage, went out and gathered together all the bicycles from the ditch where we fought and took them back to the yard, where he cut each of them in half with huge bolt cutters and left them there as a warning to the young yobbos who spoiled his day and interrupted his evening. I choose to believe the rumour.

CYCLING TO THE DENTIST, 1985

Maybe it's because I've fought my way out of the magical hinterland between childhood and adulthood, but some of the poetry has gone. Nameless, formless lusts have been replaced with more clinically accurate desires. And so the simple romance of walking has gone and it's back to the metal. Back on my bike. But I'm not grown up yet. There's still plenty of room for dreams . . . Even at the dentist's surgery.

It's always dark in the cellar, even with the lights on. I say lights; there's just a weedy bulb hanging from a cord above me and there's a small corridor off the main room that I swear soaks the light right into the gloomy Victorian brickwork like a rag mopping up oil. But I'm fifteen and clearly am not going to be afraid of the dark. My cousin Adrian once explained to me, when we were kids, how at night everything is exactly the same, it's just that you can't see so well. We were on a big family camping trip at Harewood House near Harrogate and he said it as we were making our way back to our tents from a playing field in the dark. We had to walk under a bridge where even the watery moonlight failed to wash through and, although I never said it to Adrian, I was a bit nervous. I kept think-ing about owls – they've always been a peculiar source of terror to me – and I was worried that I might hear one and not be able to stop myself screaming in front of my older, bigger cousin. But his words made so much sense and were so pragmatic and obvious and true, that they took the fear away. Obviously I'm never scared of the dark now, when I'm working down here in the cellar on my bikes – I'm fifteen, for God's sake – but I get kind of tense when I have to walk down that small corridor at the back to look for parts in one of the big wooden boxes at the very end, in the damp bit where I think they used to keep the coal. They must have done, in fact, because there's still a sort of hatch at the top where they would have tipped the coal in from a sack, and it gets very damp down there, smells bad and is simply awash with spiders. I hate spiders, not afraid to admit that, not at any age, and the horror of leaning over the edge of the crates, sweatshirt catching on old nails and splinters of wood as I reach down into the darkness to rattle around among the handlebars and mudguards and saddles and brake levers to find a part is unspeakable. Although I'm speaking it now, right, so I may as well carry on. It's horrible. I'm convinced I'm going to brush my hand against some enormous species of as yet undiscovered spider that's going to bite my hand and run up my arm to sit on my chest and watch with its cluster of cold, alien eyes as I writhe and spasm on the damp cellar floor. If I feel so much as a strand of cobweb against my palm or my fingers in the unseen depths of the crate, I snatch my arm back so quickly I risk dislocating a shoulder.

I wish I could have some music on down here in the gloom, as I fit and fix and bolt and polish. But I've got nothing to play it on, although there is a power point I could plug it into if I had; an old double socket, cream with age, at the end of a length of plastic ducting behind the cold slab I use as a workbench. It's too low really, the cold slab; it was designed to store meat and stuff in Victorian times when they didn't have fridges. The stone is a foot thick, so it always stays cold and can keep things cool. You just slapped it right on there, no door to open and no light to come on automatically either. There are stains on its smooth surface, blood I guess, from the legs of pigs or whatever they kept on it. But it's only a foot or so off the ground so I'm always having to bend right over to work on a bike frame as I grease bearings to fit a crank or try to wrestle a rusty gear lever bracket around a gauge of tubing it was never really designed to clamp around. The single worst mistake you can make in the entire world is to think, for even a moment, that it's OK to store something underneath the slab. Say I've been using that old shoe box with crank parts in, cotter pins and chain wheels and stuff, and I've finished getting the bits I want out of it and need to clear it away while I fit them to the frame of a racer. I'll need space on the slab, it's about a yard and a half wide and a yard deep, so I might think to myself, OK, I'll slide that box under the slab where there's a gap just big enough to fit it and maybe put it back up on the shelf when I've finished. So I'll slide it in – great Whitesnake song that, 'I'm gonna slide it in, right to the top ...', a stormer to play in front of Mum and Dad on the old stereo in the living room and see if they react – so anyway, I'll slide the box under the slab and then that, believe me, is the end of it. Because that little gap under the slab, that twelve-inch-high void of purest and most utter darkness that goes back a yard or so to the wall behind – except I suspect it probably doesn't, but carries on for all of eternity – is where nightmares are made. The spiders under there will have your leg off and eat it in front of you. So the box containing crank parts will fester under there along with everything else that I have, at one time or another, decided to slide under there, for all of time.

I'm rebuilding an old favourite today. This thing has been through more incarnations than Gandhi – does he go through incarnations? I dunno, but anyway, you take my point; this bike has changed a lot over the years. It's got a charcoal-black frame, well it has now, I painted it years back; I think it was blue to start with. Or yellow. Maybe both. It's actually a size or so too small for me, can't remember where I got it from, probably swapped it for something with someone. Anyway, its last incarnation was as a sort of a custom thing. This was when we lived back down south in Solihull. I'd got hold of a set of chopper bars, real high-risers like on a chopper bike, exactly like, in fact, the ones on the motorbikes on my bedroom wallpaper as a kid.

I fitted them to this frame, cinching down the bracket

on the handlebar stem as tight as I could because the 'bars were actually a slightly narrower diameter than the dropped, racer-style 'bars I'd taken out of it. Then I fitted a smaller diameter front wheel to it, one off a smaller bike so it looked even more like a chopper, with a bigger wheel at the back than the front. It meant losing the front brakes, but hey, this was a chopper and hardly about practicality. The bigger problem was that the new 'bars weren't fixed properly; they wouldn't stay upright in the handlebar stem. The tubing they were made from was too narrow for the jaws of the bracket to grip tightly enough. So I got a thin piece of tin, cut from an old biscuit-tin lid – I had to use a hammer and a cold chisel for that because I didn't have any tin snips; made a horrible mess of my right hand on the edges – and wrapped it round the base of the handlebars to act as a sleeve to make the tubing fatter and give the bracket a chance of gripping it.

I tightened the bolts until the Allen key slipped and rounded them off, then wheeled my creation out into the front garden. It looked brilliant, a proper chopper. I hung tassels from the ends of the high bars to complete the look. Well, almost. On a real chopper motorbike they would have been leather, but I had to use ribbons. Same deal though. Looked great. I set off down Ralph Road and it wasn't until I got halfway down the hill on the way to Prospect Lane shops that I tried the back brake, just to slow down a bit because it was getting a wobble on. And

75

that was when I had a horrible, hideous crash. As I braked, the extra leverage the long bars exerted on the grip of the handlebar stem bracket at the base proved way too much for the jaws to cope with and the bars folded forward, my hands rotating over the top and out over the front wheel. I followed, the bike hit the kerb and I went straight over the top as the bike's front wheel stopped dead at a low wall outside a house and I carried on, into the hedge. It didn't hurt so much as shock. It felt as if I'd died. Killed by elemental physics.

When I recovered enough to check the bike, it looked ridiculous. The 'bars had folded forward over the front wheel like big, drooping horns, giving it the appearance of a skinny bull with its head held low. I folded them back upright, easy enough now they'd slipped once, and wheeled it home to the shed. And there it stayed until we loaded it on to the lorry with all my other bike-building stuff to move house up here.

These days, choppers are way out of fashion. Everyone's riding large-framed bikes with cow-horn bars – those broad, flat bars that extend as far out to the sides as possible, so the rider has to spread his arms until his back is bent and his face is only a foot or so above the stem. And I've got a set of cow horns. Well, they're not as wide as I'd like but they're flat and sweep back like the real thing, just not as far out. I'm going to strip the frame of everything I don't need, 'cos that's the look. It needs to be pared down, simple and brutal, like a skinhead. I'll ditch the naff bottle-carrier and the shortie front mudguard and the long, rattly back one. Obviously, I'm going to put a proper-sized front wheel back in, although the small one has long since gone and the frame is lying in front of me now with just a buckled back wheel at one end and the chopper bars lying parallel to and alongside the forks.

I don't know what to do about gears. It's got a Sturmey-Archer hub set on it at the moment, the kind of system with a little chain that comes out of the hub to pull the cogs about inside and shift ratios. It's the sort of thing that belongs on a shopping bike for an old lady and has absolutely no place on this creation. If it's going to have any, they'll have to be derailleur. Certainly not a ten-speed though, even if I had a double chain wheel and front derailleur to fit it; that just smacks of trying too hard. This bike is going to be about not giving a shit, not trying to set speed records or even go fast. It'll go at whatever pace I choose. It's going to be mean and hard. I might even make it a single-speeder – not something I've ever done before, but it can't be that hard. I'll just have to shorten the chain.

★ ★ ★

I would never shorten the chain. Or finish the bike. I spent a lot of time in the damp cellar, working on it, but after three weeks of struggling to fit a derailleur hanger to the rear chain stay, cursing my own efforts to adapt brackets from old light sets or bottle-holders to work in place of the absent lugs on the tubing to hold the thing in place, I would give up in disgust. I never even saw what would have been the crowning moment: fitting those broad handlebars would have been like mounting the antlers to the head of the proudest of stags. But the bars would never be fitted and the bike would fester down there for some time, before being swapped or given away. I can't remember now and I didn't know then that the project would fail, as I surveyed the pile of parts strewn across the cold slab and resolved to make this the best bike I had ever built. And I had built a few. This was my realm, down here, my workshop. I could retreat here, hide away from the mounting pressures of burgeoning teenage-hood and toil happily among the fantasies and dreams I tried to build.

★ ★ ★

I looked around at the piles of waiting bicycle parts, at the long, drooping shelf down one wall on which were stacked damp boxes containing the smaller bits I might need to build a particular bike: chainrings and crank arms, brake levers and luggage racks. I wished it was tidier, but never seemed to find the time to tidy it, and I wouldn't have enjoyed meeting any of the thousands of huge spiders I knew to have made those tangled piles of potential their homes. Still buoyed up by this new project's progress and strengthened by my resolve to fit it out with a simple, five-gear derailleur set-up and maybe one of those medium-length rear mudguards that kick up a bit at the end, I turned for the door and the steps to the kitchen upstairs.

At the bottom of the steps my current bicycle leaned against the wall. It was a bicycle bought for me by my parents some two or three years earlier, a red Peugeot. The bike and I had suffered a traumatic early relationship, we had struggled to bond, but it was part of my life now and we worked well together. I lifted it to my shoulder, ready to climb the steep wooden stairs, more of a ladder really, out of the cellar. It wasn't a convenient set-up, carrying my bicycle down to the cellar after I had used it, only to carry it back up to go out again, but the old brick shed in the yard where I had kept it before had never really held off the rain and eventually was pulled down to make space. If I wanted to preserve the machine, and I did, then this was my best option.

I had an appointment at the dentist, a short ride across Ripon. Running errands in the interest of simple self-maintenance was one of the new things that age had brought me. I couldn't remember the precise point at which my mother had stopped coming with me to the dentist or the doctor, it had just sort of evolved and now I would have felt awkward being taken there by her. Wrestling the bike through the doorway at the top of the stairs

79

I yelled my goodbyes to the silent house and made for the back door. It was grey outside, of course, but not raining and I looked forward to the short blast into town, young leg muscles flexing in anticipation of the work to come.

I was counting the days to my sixteenth, when I hoped to get a 50cc motorcycle and launch myself into a terrifying new world of adult responsibility and impossible glamour. Within six months, as my birthday grew closer, I would be counting the hours, but right now, only fifteen years old and recently plunged into a co-ed school for the first time, my bicycle was perhaps a welcome link with my childhood, a wordless explanation to an increasingly crowded and crowding world that I was still a kid really and couldn't be blamed if I didn't understand how things worked. Not that anyone would dare blame me for anything when I took to the road on the mean and menacing project taking shape in the cellar. Grinning to myself at the prospect, I climbed on to my red racer with a trace of distaste for its childish, gleaming lines and silvery metal parts that just screamed of keenness, of trying too hard and of actually caring about stuff.

A half-mile up the road into town, in a parade of shops on the right, was the newsagent where, after a few minutes of huffing and shrugging my shoulders and practising deepening my voice, I would buy cigarettes. The brand I usually bought came in an old-fashioned pack, a sleeve with a separate insert that folded out at the top, like the flap at the end of a cardboard box, rather than the more usual flip-top. Two reasons for this: they reminded me of the packs my grandfather, long since dead of lung cancer, used to smoke; and secondly, the packet itself was smaller, making it easier to hide in a blazer pocket or pencil case. My days of slotting a single cigarette inside an over-sized fountain pen and hiding the pen at the bottom of my bag like a drug smuggler were long gone, though I sometimes missed the extra secrecy of it. I'd felt like a spy, looking for ever-more cunning hiding places for my illicit cargo. It reminded me of childhood days when my brothers and I would make walkie-talkies out of matchboxes, with one match sticking out as an aerial, and set out on deadly missions across the lawn in total and absolute secrecy, sneaking through the house, holding urgent, whispered conversations about where people were, what they were doing and how they might catch us.

I was nearly of a legal age to buy cigarettes now and that took away some of the pleasure, reducing them to something more mundane and less, well, less naughty. Rebellious would be a better word for it. Once it became legal, where would be the rebellion in it? My parents both smoked, so they could hardly complain, though I dreaded them finding out because I knew that, when they did, they wouldn't shout or scream or be cross, instead they would break out the dreaded phrase, 'We're not cross, son, we're disappointed.' And that disappointment was something I needed to avoid hearing about. It was a burden as heavy to me as the worst guilt; it hung like a thin, evil grey fog, ready to smother me before they or anyone else in authority had finished the first syllable of the word. But while I still risked parental disappointment, I knew that if the school objected to my smoking it could only be on the grounds of where I was doing it, not the fact that I was doing something illegal. I didn't need to buy any today though; I had the tail-end of a pack tucked away in the back pocket of my jeans. I told myself to remember this and move them to a different pocket before I sat down in the dentist's waiting room and ruined the three remaining smokes I had in there. I'd buy some more tomorrow, Saturday, on my way to the chicken farm where I worked weekends.

After the parade of shops, up a slight hill into town, a road off to the right took me to school. I wouldn't be taking it today, but during term time it was my daily ride. I generally rode it alone, though sometimes with friends. Riding home with my best mate, Benny, early in the year, I had committed an act of unbelievable cruelty. Leaving the school gates and heading downhill on the main road, we had both slipped naturally into a race, each pretending not to be bothered about being in front but each pumping pedals until our lungs felt ragged and our breath felt raw in our throats. We powered down the hill, no breath left for laughter but grinning wildly, hair streaming. Riding dead level with Benny, I had looked across at him and watched his face, his mouth made wider and eyes narrowed by the streaming wind. We were alongside each other, only inches apart. I heard the thin chain of his bike streaming over the gear wheels and through the derailleur. And I reached across to his handlebars and wrenched them to the right. Instantly, Benny disappeared behind me, vanishing as I streaked ahead.

As though off camera or off stage, I heard the unmistakable sound of a bicycle crash: a hollow, ringing clang circled with lighter metallic tinkles as the bike smashed into the tarmac and the dull thud of clothed limbs as Benny followed it. I heard car brakes screech as I stopped and turned to see Benny, on his hands and knees, face close to the ground, eyes tightly shut and a car stopped, barely inches from his backside. His bike lay stretched on the road like a dead thing. I breathed into the sudden silence, unsure of the what, the why and the what happens next of it all. Benny looked at me and I saw the question in his eyes. I had no answer; it was one of those uncontrollable outbursts, those impulsive, reckless actions springing from the mad, bubbling cauldron that simmered inside me.

Two years later, driving through Ripon in my first car with a girlfriend alongside, we laughed and talked dirty and, caught in the moment, desperate to do something reckless and crazy and important to prove my vigour, my potential, I took off my watch and threw it out of the window. We laughed as it fell into the traffic behind us and I saw it, in my mind, pulverised under wheels and ground into the road's surface. There was an immediate twinge of something, a sense that I would, maybe soon, regret doing it, but we laughed in the bright moment and felt we could do anything, anything we wanted, and we shared the feeling that it was incredible to be so unfettered, so free, so bursting with freshness. For a brief and infinite moment, the world wasn't frightening, it was a chessboard and we were the biggest pieces on it.

★ ★ ★

I loved being on the road by myself, taking responsibility for decisions at important places, at junctions and crossings and lights, albeit only on a bicycle. Obviously I would never have shared this with my school friends; even if I'd wanted to, I couldn't have found the words to express it. I was at that stage where moving through this adult world was still new to me and I enjoyed it for its novelty. Every street correctly identified and every stoplight duly obeyed with a theatrical sigh and an impatient shrug was one more milestone on my journey into adulthood.

Where the main streets enter the Market Place in Ripon, set back from the road in a ramshackle corner building with an anonymous door letting into a side street, was the dentist's surgery. I rolled up the kerb, slipping my right foot out

 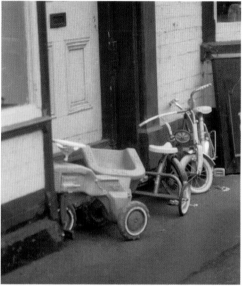

Yes, that is my pedal car. And yes, I am cleaning it.

An impossibly complex social message, right there.

Leaving on a cycling adventure with my older cousin, in, er, god, where was the style in those days?

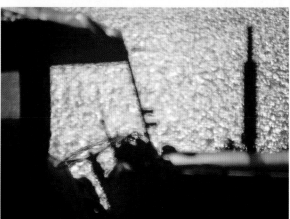

There were no PlayStations in 1982, but even if there were I would have been mooching about taking miserable pictures. At least Abbey, my Border Collie, looks happy. Ish.

Again, angst, gloom and an unerring ability to find misery in the chirpiest of situations. Yes, I was a teenager with a cheap camera and a homemade darkroom. What do you expect?

My best mate Ian and a selection of borrowed bikes at Sharrow Common, 1985. We never had permission to ride there. We never sought it. I don't know whether it would have been granted if we had done so, so it's probably as well that we didn't.

of the toe clip and let the bike tick to a stop. I had forgotten my lock; it was difficult to carry and I wasn't about to resort to a backpack, so I leaned the bike against a downpipe under a small, high frosted window next to the door and walked in, sneaking a look back at the bike and hoping it would still be there when I came out. Vinyl seats with tarnished metal legs, a small counter behind a glass screen, a coffee table bearing old magazines, a shelf of dog-eared children's books and a stout potted plant: typical waiting-room stuff. I gave my name and squeaked on to a seat.

The waiting room was empty but for one other patient. She sat opposite. Long, dark hair framed the magazine she read. The hands holding the sides of the magazine were soft and pale and she gripped it lightly, casually, between fingers and thumbs. Outside, traffic buzzed around the market square, big diesels pulled and mooed and air-brakes hissed. Judging by the clothes, she must be my age. Both feet planted on the lino floor in fashionably chunky lace-up boots, a long skirt of many colours drifted about at their tops. She brought the sides of the magazine together to turn a page and I caught the angles of her face, high cheekbones, dark eyes, and her mouth perfectly straight even though her lips were puckered, perhaps questioning what she read. She looked up, saw me and I looked down, studying my thumb. And she went on reading, while the traffic hummed outside. Feeling as if a million particles were being exchanged in the air between us, I concentrated on exuding something, some special potion of hormones and spirit that would connect us. As I watched, she dipped the magazine to peer over the top at me and smiled, the planes of her cheekbones pitched higher over her broad, full mouth under eyes like a cat's.

'Mr Hammond.' A nurse at the brown-painted door alongside the counter called my name. I blushed and stood, remembering too late the remaining cigarettes in my back pocket, and turned to the door. I risked a look back at the girl in the chair; she was still smiling and as she lifted the magazine back up, her eyebrows raised with it.

I wasn't scared of the dentist. Far from it: I enjoyed the attention. Well, I enjoyed the attention given to my teeth. I was the patient and the needs of my teeth came first, but I wasn't expected to do anything. I liked the fact that I was just a spectator, there only to bring my mouth with me and then lie still while it was worked on. I was a transportation device for my teeth, nothing more. Compared with the ordeal of sitting in front of a mirror and trying not to blush for the interminable self-conscious hours it took to cut my hair, a visit to the dentist was a breeze. And I enjoyed the opportunity to be brave, not to wince or shrink away from the bright, hard-chromed tools. I might occasionally allow a little narrowing of the eyes or a twitch of a hand to let the pretty dental nurse know it hurt but that I wasn't making a fuss about it. Staring up at the bright light, I thought about the girl in the waiting room while the dentist, face hidden behind his paper mask, rattled and scraped my teeth.

She was beautiful. I felt her eyes on me still as I lay in the chair. I pictured her standing alongside the dentist, looking, watching, smiling. Her smile fizzed with contained energy. Was it mischief? Was she a bad girl? And if so, how were 'bad girls' actually bad? How did this badness manifest itself and what wouldn't I give to be there when it did? At fifteen, most of my waking time, or at least that part of it not spent thinking about cars and bikes, was spent thinking about girls. Sometimes in the simplest, basest terms, but often in a painful, whimsical, keening way. I lusted, yes, but I lusted for connection, for a meeting of souls too. I had little or no experience of actually sating these desires with a real, actual girl. And I couldn't imagine one ever being willing to comply with my own shameful urges, let alone actually enjoy the process. It was, as far as I could see, an insurmountable obstacle. Girls were to be captured by the brave, won by champions with limitless reserves of confidence. I shied away from them still, only just settled into a co-ed school after years spent in a boys' school where it was easy to consider girls as objects of lust and desire without ever having to actually engage with one except in my imagined fumblings and erotic rompings.

Her face floated in front of me, conjured up in the dentist's bright light above my head. We would walk by the river, I decided. The would be a romantic soul, in touch with nature, a girl of the wild. Her hand would slip naturally into mine, we would draw closer as we walked and then would sit down by the river where I would uncover the mysteries, the warmth, the velvety textures, limbs, curves and intersections beneath that long skirt and finally be transported to join the fellowship of those who have conquered that insurmountable barrier to share their barely containable physicality with another. For reasons of discretion I decided to change the course of my thoughts as I lay on the chair under the ministrations of the dentist and his nurse. But still, the wild girl loitered in the dark corners of my mind and I struggled to keep her at bay.

★ ★ ★

She wasn't there. The waiting room was empty. Only the potted plant loomed, green and ugly in a corner. Of course she wasn't there. Thoughts of encounters on riverbanks by knotted tree roots ebbed and flowed along with earthier lusts and tangled notions. Maybe it wasn't to be. But hold on, I had gone into my dentist first and my treatment had only been for a filling: quick, in and out in ten minutes. The girl would still be in with her dentist, in another bright-lit room. I tried to imagine this creature of the forest, this earthbound angel, lying on the technical chair in the antiseptic confines of a dentist's surgery

... and I couldn't. But I could imagine her stepping out again. I would wait. However I couldn't just stand there in the waiting room, hands in pockets, and wait for her. So I left, walking down the two stone steps to the pavement to lift my bicycle, still there, away from the rusty black downpipe.

Leaning the bike against my leg I pulled my packet of cigarettes from my back pocket. Ruined: all of them mashed and misshapen. Of the three in there, just a stump remained usable. I stuck the surviving half a cigarette in my mouth quickly, a sudden sense that she was close making my hands dart and shake. My grey plastic Clipper lighter worked and soon the ragged ends of the broken stump were rounded into the uniformity of the burn. I drew deeply on it, the smoke tasting of bitter leaves against the dentist's minty mouthwash. With one hand, I carefully leaned my bike back against the wall. I held the little grey lighter in my other hand. I wished I had a brass Zippo with a sprung lid to snap shut. I had a fake one once; it was too shiny to be genuine and the flint wheel wasn't properly fixed on its spindle, but it worked and made a satisfying noise when I closed it, and it felt good in my pocket. When it ran out of fuel I had tied a piece of string to it and dipped it in a can of petrol at Benny's house. Thumbing the wheel afterwards, instead of the explosive inferno I expected, nothing happened. It never worked again and I either lost it or gave it away or swapped it. I tucked the Clipper away in my pocket, leaving my hand in there with it. She would be out soon.

The traffic was building up as the afternoon slid by. My single cigarette burned down and I stamped the stub on to the pavement. If I couldn't be leaning against the downpipe smoking moodily, I would give her the impression that I was just leaving, my appointment only just over and that it was chance, or fate, that led me to be there at the door when she appeared. I lifted the bike away from the wall and half wheeled, half carried it to the kerb and on to the road. I climbed on, my weight resting on my left leg and my right hooked up on to the pedal, ready to leave. This was the perfect pose, absolutely ready to go. A horn sounded on the other side of the Market Place. There was no market on today but people were moving across its broad, stone expanse under the shadow of Ripon's famous Obelisk, rushing to cars to go home. I looked down at my right foot and, with my toe, rotated the rat-trap pedal so that the toe clip was upright, its steel loop and frayed black nylon belt open and ready to receive. The toe clips were a later addition of my own; the bike hadn't had any when I got it. They had cost me a lot but they transformed the bicycle in my eyes and were an important part of our bonding process, a small modification made by me, like a bad habit broken in a long-term partner or a different haircut insisted upon. She wouldn't be impressed with toe clips. Or would she? Ah fuck it, she's never coming out. I'm off.

RIPON TO SHARROW COMMON ON HONDA MTX 50, 1986

This was it, I had a key. A key I coud grab from the kitchen table
and use to start my engine and then I could just take off, go,
wherever I chose. This was freedom on an unimaginable scale.
Traffic lights, junctions, Speed limits, they all played a part in my
life now. Even if only as distant targets. I could see the engine
working in my mind, could taste the pulses of air and petrol rushing
into the combustion chamber and feel the piston being driven down
the bore by the explosions within.

This was months after my bike had first arrived in my world, a lopsided dream, leaning with casual defiance against the yard wall, as cool and loose-shouldered as a cowboy propped against a bar. We had bonded by now, the bike and I, and so I began the journey with the same careless abandon that lesser mortals might set off on foot to the newsagents; at least, that is how I wanted it to look. In truth, I was nervous. Still timid about the process of climbing aboard the bike and kicking it into life to merge into the real, adult world of traffic lights, traffic jams and policemen, and more nervous still about the destination. Ian would be ready, waiting for me at his house, and we would set off together from there for Sharrow Common, where kids like us gathered informally to ride their dirt bikes around a course set into the muddy dips and rises of a patch of apparently unowned scrubland. We never had permission to ride there. We never sought it. No one ever did. I don't know if it would have been granted had we done so, so it's probably as well that we didn't.

My bike was a red Honda MTX50. And just typing it and seeing it there has raised my pulse. It meant everything to me. I'm not overstating its significance; I defined myself by this machine and would have melded myself with it physically so that we became fused into one bio-mechanical whole like a sort of Star Trek Borg character – if the Borg were made up of half an old red motor-cycle and half a sixteen-year-old with hair slightly too long for the headmaster's approval but not so long as to upset his grandmother who lived in the dining room. But Borg technology was not freely available in Ripon, North Yorkshire, in 1986. Probably still isn't – though you never know; Northern market towns like Ripon have an intensity to them and can be multi-layered places with many a secret fizzing away beneath the 'Town in Bloom' tourist veneer. I know for a fact there was a transvestite there. Well, probably not an actual transvestite, but he was quite an effeminate old man and we used to see him in the town's many pubs, drinking alone but always happy to chat to us while we pretended to be eighteen and to like beer. There was a rumour that he'd once kicked hell out of two squaddies from the nearby camp for being rude to him. So we were always nice and polite. I'm sure he once had blue eyeshadow on.

I kept the bike in the yard behind our smart Victorian

terrace. We lived in one of those houses that looks from the front like a pretty substantial place, all very Upstairs Downstairs, but, unknown to the passing admirer, it narrows towards the back until, at the end of the yard behind the house, it was only as wide as the gate. They were just big show-offs, the Victorians: all front and no trousers. The broad bars of my Honda just fitted through the gate and I would test myself by not getting off to push the bike into the yard. I had to stand on the pegs and ride it. A couple of times the rubber end of the handlebar grip grazed the bricks on either side, but I figured it was the sort of low-speed, precision practice that great riders founded their future success on. I looked forward to telling Michael Parkinson about it one day.

★ ★ ★

I got my bike (I savour the phrase still; it feels good in my mouth, 'my bike' – like saying 'my dragon', 'my laser rifle', 'my Oscar') when I was sixteen. And I don't mean sometime in the year when I was sixteen, I mean on the day I reached sixteen. Had I been a more confident, ballsy kid, I would have set out on to the cold, midnight streets as the second hand first ticked on to the hour I came of age. As it was, I didn't like to wake the family and getting up early would have set the dog off barking, so instead I had lain in bed in a fury of childish anticipation and watched the minutes pass until I could head downstairs, acknowledge the cards and best wishes from my parents and brothers, force a Weetabix down my neck and set out on the single most exciting, enticing and exhilarating endeavour this newly minted sixteen-year-old had ever dreamed of.

Sixteen is the age at which the law decreed a person was mature enough to take over the controls of a 'machine limited to 50 kmh (30 mph) and with an engine of no more than 50cc capacity'. It was the age at which a person cast off the state of being helpless, stranded wherever he had last been put by his parents or family friends. His bicycle no longer represented the limit of his ability to find a place in the world; he was free to roam its furthest reaches. He no longer represented a burden, a cargo of ballast to be dutifully transported about the place by his parents. I. Was. Free.

★ ★ ★

If I've made myself sound like a spoiled kid by saying I got my bike on the day I was sixteen, I need to clear that up. This was not a new bike. Not by a long, long way. It was already ancient. It leaned against the wall in our yard because the side stand was broken, sheared off at the top, leaving a useless two-inch stub and I could no more afford to replace it than I could buy a super yacht. I wasn't one of those kids who got given everything he wanted and everything his mates had. Not for me a Raleigh Chopper, a Six Million Dollar Man, a BMX, a skateboard, a Rubik's Cube or an Atari. If I sound bitter, I don't mean to. All I wanted was a motorcycle. And I got one, so none of the other shit mattered. The bike cost £200. I paid half of it myself, out of my wages from the chicken farm where I worked weekends between weekdays spent at school. Mum and Dad paid the other half as my birthday present. So yes, I was a bit spoiled. In fact, the bigger indulgence, rather than paying for it, was in letting me have it at all. Parents in the 1980s generally didn't relish the idea of their kids having bikes.

This was when motorcycles still stood for something. There was a whiff of counter-culture about them and they were demonised in public information films on telly when an unfortunate bloke in washed-out colours would be knocked off his Honda Superdream by some inattentive nelly in a Ford Escort and lie there on the road, all dead but with no blood pooling around him, while we looked on in awe and horror over our Lego or cup of Typhoo and, depending on our standpoint, wondered either a) how we would ever persuade our parents to let us have a bike, or b) how in hell we would make sure none of our three sons ever threw a leg over one of those death machines.

Thing was, I had dreamed of a bike for over ten years. Dad and I had worked out, when I was about five, how many days it would be until I could take my driving test.

It was many, many days, but I diligently began counting them off. Then I discovered I could ride a bike a full 365 days earlier than I could drive a car. And so my obsession began. And with each year that went by, each excited proclamation that it was now only 1825, or 1460, or 1095, or 730, or 365 days until I could ride a bike, my parents' doom grew more certain. They hadn't grasped that their only option was to quash the idea the moment it was born, when the tally of days was still in the high three thousands. But they didn't quash it. It grew and with each passing year its looming promise became more fundamental to who I was and who I wanted to be. When the time came, as we hit the ramp up to my actual sixteenth birthday and the approaching dawn of a reality I had dreamed about daily for most of my life as a sentient, talking human being, they could no more deny me a bike than they could cut my head off.

It was old and it looked old. As the weeks went by I cleaned it every day and it did start to look better, though still obviously old. The seat bore the high gloss burnished on to it by the jeans of God only knew how many other teenagers who had ridden the bike into adulthood and freedom. The bar grips, scuffed by me on the rough bricks either side of the impossibly narrow entrance to our yard, already had chunks missing, as though mice had nibbled at the broad, rubber flange where the grip ended and gave way to the brake and clutch lever assemblies. Astride it,

I marvelled at the size of the Honda. Sure, I wasn't a big kid, but this was a big bike for a fifty – a fifty being a 50cc motorcycle, or more accurately, a motorcycle with a cylinder capacity of not exceeding 49 cubic centimetres, the smallest manufactured, and the only option available to us sixteen-year-old riders. We had talked of 'fifties' and nothing else, not even girls, over the past year as my best mate Ian and I made our final, breathless approach to the most important landmark anniversary we would ever attain.

One of the plastic side panels had split away from the bolt mounting it to the frame and hung off limply. I had to reattach it each time I rode the bike; hooking it back over the mounting bolt and pressing it into place with a slowly disintegrating piece of tape. The irregularity annoyed me, but replacing it with a new panel was an expensive option I had never even bothered looking into. What annoyed me even more was that this panel that caused me so much bother as a constant, physical reminder of my bike's tatty state and my wallet's feeble powers was the only one bearing the legend 50cc and as such, the only betrayer of my bike's diminutive capacity and, by association, of my young age and lowly status. In every other respect, my beloved, if tired companion looked to be bigger and more substantial than a 50cc moped. I was caught then, in a permanent and dreadful quandary: keep fixing the panel back on, which meant revealing to the world the truth about my bike and my age, or disguise the facts by letting it drop off. But then I'd be riding around with the battery and its attendant wires exposed. Unthinkable. So it stayed, hanging on by its weather-worn piece of tape and requiring refixing before, after and often during every trip.

On a day forever scorched into my memory, an older kid had approached Ian and me as we went about the ritual of pulling on gloves and helmets. We had been sitting on our bikes on the Market Place in Ripon, watching the world go by and sneering and trying to look cool without appearing as though we were trying to look cool. It was hard. I couldn't lean the bike over on its side stand and slump on it like a casually italicised rebel without a cause because the side stand had snapped off. So I had to sit with it upright between my legs and support it with my feet, which only just touched the ground, constantly alert for the slightest breath of wind that could knock me over. It didn't help either that my leather jacket – bought for £5 from my mate, Eddie, who had kept it, judging by the smell, in his cowshed – was split along the seam under my left arm. I teamed this draughty, whiffy symbol of rebellion with a pair of enormous, pseudo-off-road boots bought from the bargain clearance shop in town for £7. They featured huge red plastic representations of, I think, tyre tread down the front. I'm not sure they were really bike boots at all, but they were the closest I could get and with my jeans tucked into their tops they looked, to my mind, better than Ian's trainers at any rate.

The kids approaching us were older, probably seven-teen. A fact confirmed by a glance across at their bikes; both 125cc jobs, a chunky red XL125 off-roader – four-stroke engine, its bigger, deeper boom sounding like a spitfire to my ears when it ran – and a sleek, low-slung Kawasaki AR125 road bike. The AR wasn't wear-ing an 'L' plate, which meant either that the rider had passed his bike test – putting him several leagues beyond our humble status – or couldn't be arsed to obey the law and display one. Either way, by dint of superior age or lawlessness, these guys were cooler than us with our crappy kit, puny 50cc bikes and huge, flappy, law-abiding L plates.

'That a one seventy-five?' the skinny one said without looking at me.

'No. It's er, it's a . . .' and as I tried to frame the word 'fifty' the significance of what this lanky stranger had just said roared through my mind. He'd said 'one seventy-five'. Not 'fifty', not even 'one twenty-five'. He said 'one seventy-five'. I didn't even know if you could get a Honda MTX with a 175cc engine, but the fact was this proper bike-riding guy, this lawless, gutsy rebel standing in front of me now with nicotine-yellow fingers and an old green bomber jacket slumped round his skinny shoulders had assumed my bike to be not one, but two sizes above where it really stood in the pecking order. I didn't like to tell him the truth; I'd rather leave him thinking he'd chatted to a

101

bloke on a Honda MTX175 and that that bloke was me, on my bike.

'... it's a fifty,' I muttered under my breath, compelled by upbringing to deliver the truth, even if only quietly, and I looked at Ian. His generous face wore the joy only a true mate could feel when his comrade and not himself had been given such a blessing, such a life-affirming gift as this. Without saying another word to the older guy, we crammed our helmets on, ran straps through the D-rings to fasten them, forced cold hands into creaky gloves, turned down fuel taps to 'on', stamped on kick-starts, pulled in clutches, selected first gear with delicate, foot-operated gear levers, revved and screamed off in a blue cloud of burned two-stroke oil and total teenage joy to howl the good news with the frantically firing pistons in our engines that we were adults now, that we had a place in the world and that we were coming for you, coming for you all and you'd better watch out.

But what did we have to say to those adults? How exactly would we take them on? We didn't know. Really, not a clue. And isn't that the point of teenage rebellion? We were angry at the world because we were teenagers. Maybe our anger grew out of fear or bubbled up because we felt stifled, held back right on the verge of adulthood. Whatever the root of it, if you're angry, you want to shout. And what better way to shout than with an engine, bowing to the command of your clenched teenage fist gripping the throttle?

To be fair, this was a pretty mild teenage rebellion. We couldn't even go fast. A 50cc – or more correctly, 49cc – motorcycle is very, very limited in power. With its tiny thimble of a piston pumping as fast as it absolutely could it was able to produce a measly 2.5 bhp. That's not a lot. A modern-day Kawasaki ZZR1400, which is just a bigger, newer motorcycle for bigger, older kids, produces nearly 200 bhp. And a Bugatti Veyron comes in at 1000 bhp – but then it's a £1.5 million VW Golf for the impossibly wealthy and tasteless and is as interesting and dangerous to drive as an Ikea sofa. The point is, Ian and I weren't roaring into our battle with the adult world bearing any particularly significant arms. Even a garden lawnmower boasts 6 bhp, two or three times what our bikes had, and I don't think anyone has ever been scared of or intimidated by someone with a lawnmower. Apart from moles, perhaps. I imagine it's pretty scary and intimidating – inconvenient, actually – to have your house levelled in seconds by a huge, screaming machine the size of an entire row of houses. I sometimes mow round molehills because I feel bad at the thought of squashing them. But I always go back and get them at the end; they ruin the lawns. It's funny, isn't it, I wouldn't mind looking out of my windows at owls nesting in the oak trees, bears emerging, bleary-eyed and hungry, from hibernation in a rough, underground den at the bottom of my garden, or a young mother doe creeping, anxious and full of tender urgency towards the rhododendron bush by the shed to tend to her delicate fawn in the nest she had built to hide and protect it. I'd be honoured, in fact, that these creatures had chosen to share my garden with me. But show me a molehill's muddy little peak rising above the green baize and I fly into a howling fury of spittle and rage and look around for dealers in machine guns and napalm.

I hadn't yet learned to care about lawns and molehills when I took over ownership of my 50cc motorcycle and finally became a biker. I had stared at and studied bikes for over ten years by this time and could recognise anything on the road from the tiniest of details and the weirdest of angles. Nobody had ever been impressed by this. I called out the make, model and engine capacity of every single bike we passed on the long, family drives down to visit grandparents in Weston-super-Mare, or to look at 'interesting' things in Stratford-upon-Avon and my parents and brothers resolutely refused to make the impressed gasps and awestruck oohs I thought the feat demanded. But I pressed on anyway. 'Honda CBX1000, six cylinders – imagine that, SIX cylinders. It's like a wall of engine coming at you. Look at it. There, look, pulling out behind the tanker, BMW R1000RS, you can tell by the shorter fairing. The Saint rode one once, in gold. Oh, Kawasaki GPZ900R, gooorgeous' – one would appear some years later in *Top Gun*, propelling Tom Cruise and his sunglasses up a runway. But the film wasn't out yet – to be fair, I haven't seen it to this day – and neither my parents nor my brothers would express the slightest interest in the facts, let alone my incredible feat of recognition and recall. Had I been calling out the Latin names and favoured habitats of birds, no doubt someone in the car would have been impressed. Had I been able to name a footballer, his team, and his hairdresser simply from a snap glimpsed on the cover of a magazine in a newsagent as we passed, I'm sure some of my school friends would have been impressed – even my brothers might have given me a nod. I pressed on though, despite their ignorance and lack of enthusiasm, calling out every bike, even if only glimpsed peeking out from behind a truck following us, before roaring past, belching smoke and fury and reminding everyone watching why bikes and bikers were the devil's work and fixing ever more deeply into my soul the yearning desire for one.

And now I had one. It called to some crucial, elemental part of me. It still does. When I walk into my garage today as a forty-three-year-old father of two with a penchant for Scrabble and an account at Countrywide feed suppliers, and pat the gleaming black flanks of my Kawasaki ZZR1400 – the most powerful production motorcycle in the world – it stirs something deep, deep down inside

105

me, far removed from sort codes and emails and Facebook and politics. That sounds naff, I know, and if it makes you laugh, fine by me. I laugh at people sometimes too, when I don't understand what they are doing or feeling, when I don't share their joys, when they make me nervous or I feel I'm missing something. It's OK, that's how we cope with stuff. Really, I'm not trying to sell the idea of bikes and biking. Frankly, I'd rather you didn't take it up if you haven't already. There are enough of us out there. What's to be gained from another joining in? Nothing, is what. It only waters the thing down for those of us who got in earlier.

Every time another stockbroking ponce on an adventure bike he bought last week tackles the north face of Kensington to get to the City on their over-specced, over-equipped, over-sized Paris–Dakar rally-ready BMW, a tiny piece of bikelore and myth is chipped away and a Hell's Angel somewhere dies. Every time some idiot who bought a Yamaha R1 super bike because he couldn't afford a Ferrari and wanted something he could claim was the fastest thing outside the bar goes on and on to his bored mates about the time he out-dragged some guy in a Lamborghini on Park Lane and saw the guy's face and he looked really pissed off and surprised – really, while sitting in front of him on a bloody sports bike with his arse in the air and his face in the clocks, he saw the driver's face? – I want to strap him to the back of a leaky, dangerous old

GPZ and force him on a week-long tour of the Lake District until his stupid leather race suit, bought to match his bike, shrinks and he finds his knackers at the back of his throat. Boast about that then, tubby, see how impressed the guys down the golf club are when you pull up in your company Mondeo instead of on your bike, sitting on a rubber ring 'cos they've only just managed to pull your 'nads out of your chuff and it still hurts. I didn't take up riding as an alternative to golf or joining the bloody gym. I started precisely because all those people didn't ride. I wanted to be on the outside of society looking in and not to be yet one more tiresome, boastful, over-insured, firm-handshaking member of a late-to-biking, let's-stick-lunch-on-the-company-credit-card, Johnnie-come-lately, biker/accountants gang.

It still gets me fired up then, this biker thing. And that's good. And that fire was better, not surprisingly, when we were sixteen: a little more fiery and unreasonable and furious, as rage needs to be if it is to be truly enjoyed. Take a hormone-charged, jittery teenage boy, add a bike and just enough money from a weekend job collecting chickens' eggs to pay for a litre of fuel a week, and you have yourself a regular whirlwind of fury and rage and magnificence. And it was unquenchable too, this force that came through me. It didn't wane even when I was overtaken by an old lady on a bicycle as I paddled the Honda up a hill in Harrogate, my 2.5 horsepower having proved themselves not quite up to the task, leaving me with no option but to push the bike along with my feet, which is pretty tricky when you can barely touch the ground. But it was shame- and humiliation-proof, this teenage fury, all caught up in my little red bike. It didn't bother Ian and me that we weren't especially good at biking either. Being good at things was for the nerds who told their stories on TV on *Why Don't You?*, talking about collecting stuff or racing their stupid, rich-kid go-karts. We didn't need to be good at riding, we just needed to be able to get on and ride. We had bikes. We were untouchable, uncatchable. Assuming you couldn't travel faster than thirty miles an hour.

Of course, before bursting the dam of my teenage rebellion, before impressing an older kid on the market square with my MTX '175' and before setting off to meet Ian and head to Sharrow Common, I'd had to learn at least the basics of riding the thing.

★ ★ ★

I knew what to do, I had read the books and dreamed about little else for years. Trouble was, I'd never actually met anyone who had ridden a bike. My dad's more of a car bloke. My mum hadn't got a clue and my brothers are younger than me, so what the hell could they possibly know. None of my friends had ridden a bike; they were all waiting for me to roar up doing just that. And it's not like

I had to take a driving test before hitting the road. That was the point of a 50cc. Get to the magic age, sixteen years old, and away you went. I didn't know whether some sort of latent knowledge inherent to the human state was supposed to stir in me and wake on the day of my sixteenth birthday, but I had felt nothing stirring apart from a cold, squirty feeling in my tummy as I looked at my glorious red steed leaning against the wall outside in the yard. Someone had let the dog out for a poo the previous evening without walking her to the nearby fields or clearing up afterwards. The resulting little brown Mr Whippy curled perkily next to the bike's knobbly front tyre. It looked in need of a few flies buzzing around it, but none would come. It was 19 December 1985 and far too cold for flies. Dad did me the service of pretending not to notice the little fresh poo in the yard and suppressed his fury, presumably, until I had roared off into the world to begin my adult life. It may have been my imagination, but I felt a mixture of innocent expectation spiced with a swirl of cynical doubt come to the boil despite the chill in our little brick-walled yard as me, Mum, Dad and brothers Andy and Nick stood looking at the bike and ignoring the turd.

I can't remember if I spoke. I'd like to have said, 'Right then, let's get this baby on the road and do some damage to the world.' I didn't. Neither did I stride up to the bike, hoik it upright and throw a leg over it muttering, 'Right then, bitch, you're mine, now let's ride.' I'd have liked to

– that was the sort of moment my hormone-addled young mind craved. In the version in my head, I spoke the words through clenched teeth before stabbing the kick-start into life with a cowboy boot and wheelie-ing out into the big wide world, flipping the bird over my retreating shoulder to my horror-struck but admiring family as I went.

I found being a teenager frustrating. Maybe we all do. I liked rock music, hated pop, was entirely and permanently broke and didn't have a clue about clothes, was terrified of girls and had never developed acne, which seemed so intrinsic to the teenage experience of the movies and TV sitcoms that I wondered privately if something was wrong with me. I craved those multi-coloured, blistering explosions of teenage fluids erupting over my mush like the millions I saw on the faces around me, the pustules' owner somehow rendered more mature by their manifold badges of hormonal chaos. My peachy cheeks remained velvety smooth and as free of pustular pride as they were, sadly, of manly whiskers. So I grew my hair until the deputy head teacher sent me home to get it cut on the first day of the new school term. That, at least, had been cool. I told my friends that he'd caned me for good measure before sending me off. He hadn't. But the bike, the bike would grant me something physical, real and solid to establish my standing. It was a metal badge of my maturity that I could park, actually park in the school car park. The very fact that I had need of the car park would set me above even the most pus-studded of sixteeners with their fancy spots, their breaking voices and their armpit hair.

All I had to do was learn how to ride it. And I did. It went exactly like it said in the book. I turned the ignition on, my fingers fizzing with sparks as they gripped and turned the silvery key – this was a key, an ignition key that I now owned, that I would have to look after and lose and chase, shouting 'Where are my keys?' into the hall. For the time being though, I turned the key and watched as the dash lights lit up. Red for oil – that one would go out once it was started – and green for neutral. This told me that the gearbox was in neutral and the bike wouldn't shoot off up the yard and through the window into the dining room where my grandmother lived when I kicked it over. I was nervous and pulled the clutch lever in with my left hand, managing, at least, to savour the smooth movement of it as I made sure this would not end in disaster. My parents and my brothers were still looking on with bird-like fascination at this new thing unfolding in their backyard, and they definitely weren't likely to leave off staring any time soon. I half sat, half stood astride the bike, my weight on my toes and my backside resting lightly on the same spot worn to a shine by the backsides of all the other, equally charged and, probably, nervous young cowboys who had gone through this same procedure on this very bike in years gone by.

Glancing down at it, the kick-starter was slender and

small, a thin metal rod, bent at an angle. But its significance in my dreams over the preceding years meant it held the promise of the longed-for fanfare to the beginning of the rest of my life as a biker. It had once been painted as red as the fuel tank but most of the red had worn away leaving a silvery, burnished finish after thousands of kicks from teenage boots. Nobody spoke as I turned the starter so that the bit where you put your foot stuck out perpendicular to the shaft of it and to the bike's suddenly vast flanks. Hefting the bike over slightly and bracing my left leg to take all my weight and support the bike, I rested my right foot on the angled portion of the lever, feeling it drop slightly as the machinery inside meshed and shafts rested against cogs, ready to turn the engine over.

This was a two-stroke engine with a reed valve. When I kicked it – and it wouldn't be for a moment or two yet – the piston would first be pushed up the cylinder bore by the crankshaft's rotation, creating a vacuum in the crankcase below it. This would draw in the life-giving mixture of air and petrol through the reed valve, a simple flap covering a hole in the side of the crankcase. As the kick continued to turn the crankshaft, the piston would be drawn down the cylinder bore again, forcing the fuel-and-air mixture through narrow passageways and up into the cylinder above it. The piston would then make one more return journey, back up the bore, pulling a fresh supply of fuel and air into the crankcase and squashing the existing supply of fuel and air up into the top of the cylinder. This super-explosive compressed mix would then be detonated by a single, infinitesimally brief spark across the gap in the spark plug.

Seen close, it would be beautiful: the oil-slick, shiny surfaces of the crankshaft turning in the roller bearings to push the great conrod up, like a nodding donkey pump dipping its great head to draw oil from a Texan well, sending the piston, encircled like Saturn by its glittering rings, up the smooth, darkly shining walls of the cylinder towards the very top. The cratered, blackened surface of the piston's head disappears into the dark recesses at the very top of the bore, like a moon pressing up under a lightless sky. The compressed gases, squashed between this moon and this sky, vibrate with increasing intensity until the piston hits the magical Top Dead Centre. Then there's a tiny, tiny pause. A breath. A glance. Everything is held at its most potent, bursting with life. It's in the timing now, the moment when the charge of electricity is sent singing along the high tension wire and into the spark plug. I imagine a single tick, as of a modest but eternally efficient Swiss clock on a train station wall. And then, the spark plug's central electrode, until now a tiny, sterile, lifeless metal cylinder, gives birth to a vivid blue spark. The spark arches and crackles across the gap; physics, like instinct, drawing it to the curved embrace of the ground electrode. And that flash, that fraction of a second of vivid, crackling,

113

raw energy, triggers another, bigger birth as it ignites the compressed mixture of air and petrol in the dark chamber.

The exploding gases expand powerfully and quickly. There is no way out; the only option is to push the piston back down the barrel and, like a heart beating slowly before gaining confidence and rhythm as it feels its own vitality and power, the piston hits its lower limit, the connecting rod loops through the bottom of its turn on the crankshaft and the piston is pushed, with the brutal, unrelenting inevitability of physics, back up the cylinder barrel by the crankshaft's momentum, recharging the crankcase with fresh fuel and compressing the next mixture of gases in the top of the cylinder as it does so, before another tiny spark ignites the gases once more and sends it back down and it finds that essential rhythm and repeats the process again and again and again and again and again, maybe nine thousand times in a single minute. That's nearly one hundred and fifty times a second – enough to take a young boy out of his backyard and into the broad plains, pains, sins and joys of adulthood.

★ ★ ★

And now, perhaps a bit further from being a boy but no closer to adulthood, I readied myself and my bike for the trip to Sharrow Common. Today we were going dirt-bike riding. It sounded like something out of my well-leafed

Motorcycle Maintenance Manual in which black-and-white photos showed men old enough to be my grandfather working on immaculate machines with perfect spanners. In one, the bike was mounted on a special lifting ramp, raising the machine to an easier height to work on it. Ian and I would laugh for hours at the idea that anyone in this world could afford not only a brand-new bike of probably 250cc capacity, but a ramp to put it on to save bending down when you oiled the chain. We couldn't afford chain oil. And my toolkit was a throwback to my bicycle days – an empty puncture-repair-kit tin holding a plastic-handled mini-screwdriver from a Christmas cracker and a box spanner offering a selection of metric sizes, each rounded to an almost perfect circle.

Ian was my best mate and lived with his mum in a bungalow on a small estate three miles out of town. The plan was that I would ride there and then the pair of us would set off in convoy for the Common and whatever muddy mayhem awaited us there. The trip to Ian's place would be simple enough: up Palace Road – the road I lived on – and turn right. I could handle right turns easily, my years of practice on a bicycle had proven their worth from the first time I tried it on my motorcycle. But I felt the heightened sense of anticipation and the odd, slightly out-of-key sense of grating reluctance that accompanies me even now on any venture that makes me nervous.

The roads were dark and damp with autumn rain, and

I knew from experience what this would do to the grip afforded by the old, knobbly tyres of my bike. Sometimes, riding in the rain, I felt I could see the tyres touching the surface, their shining black knobbles, designed to dig in and find purchase in soft mud, suddenly looking like glossy Lego bricks, ready to skitter across the wet road and send me into a hedge. Or worse, a lamppost. Over the last few months I had suddenly noticed the looming importance of what I had heard referred to somewhere as 'Street Furniture'. I liked the phrase. It meant lampposts, signs, bollards and stuff, but I enjoyed the domestic, homely feel of it. It put me in mind of a street full of occasional tables and armchairs, and brought with it a suggestion that to those of us most vulnerable to the devastating effects of a collision with a hard, unforgiving steel sign pole or the jagged leading edge of an Armco barrier, these things were, nevertheless, just furniture. To us bikers, these hazards were armchairs and the street our living room.

The bike fired third kick; once the atmosphere in the cramped, dark confines of the cylinder reached the optimum state for ignition, the spark plug's minuscule flash was enough to explode it and send the piston straight into a fast, fluttering heartbeat.

I loved this moment. As always, I saw it unfold in my mind and savoured the inevitability, the naturalness of it. This was physics, stuff doing what it was supposed to do, what it had no choice but to do if the conditions were right.

There were times when I felt like Frankenstein, standing back as the lightning conductors fired life into his simple, doomed creation, but on this occasion I smiled with relief and satisfaction as the harsh, tinny bark bounced off the brick walls of the yard. I revved it, ostensibly to warm the engine but mostly because I liked the noise, the banshee wail and ill-tempered mutterings as the revs rose and fell. Bugger. Should have turned it to face the gate before I got on and started it. Now I was pointing back at the house, the bike's small headlight playing watery yellow beams against the stout Yorkshire brickwork under my grandmother's window.

Her curtains were closed. They usually were. I liked my grandmother, mostly because she secretly approved of my long hair and would compliment me on it when I sat with her on the floral sofa in her room and the dog scrounged malted milk biscuits as we drank tea. She liked the bike too. She had a fading black-and-white photograph of her riding pillion on one, when Grandad was alive and young, back when the motorcycle had yet to evolve from a cheap and utilitarian mode of transport into a demonic symbol of rebellion and freedom. When Nan had first shown me the picture, browned and curled, I looked at their faces, expressions open as the photograph was taken but closed off now by the huge span of time, and wondered what they were thinking and planning. Did they swear? Smoke? Were they gripped by lusts and jealousies and ambition?

117

Ever drink themselves sick on cheap lager? Did they know how it felt to be rejected, accepted, admired or ignored? And was any of that caught up and set into metal by the bike sitting obediently underneath them? I had a sneaking suspicion that she liked the rebellious streak that bikes had evolved over the decades since the photograph was taken, their new role as a symbol of naughtiness and their status as purveyors of freedom and independence. Snippers of apron strings.

My grandmother seemed to have a particular understanding of the transition from boyhood to manhood and often when we talked there would be an unexpected and surprising twinkle in her eyes. I felt that as we shared stories and news of the day and went through the niceties of a chat between grandmother and grandson, she understood what was really going on, what went through my fevered teenage mind. She probably knew too, that it was all just silly, teenage stuff, that I was in the grip of something bigger and beyond me and that it just amounted to so much hot air in the long run. I would turn out OK and she knew I would. Our grandmothers are wise, perhaps, even when they're not trying to be. Even if only because we need them to be. But right now, my bike was facing the wrong way and the narrow gate stood open behind me. Sitting down for tea, a chat and a malted milk biscuit with my grandmother was about the furthest thing from my mind.

I began to heft the bike round, reluctant to get out of the saddle. This meant paddling it backwards and forwards to make a many-pointed turn through 180 degrees. My breath bounced back hot from the chinguard of my crash helmet, warming my cold nose and misting up the visor. Eventually I would learn to avoid a fogged visor by leaving it open as I exerted myself starting and manoeuvring the bike, and, on damp days, flicking it open a crack as I pulled up to stop at junctions or to crawl through queuing cars. Later still I would learn the value of a tiny smear of washing-up liquid spread over the inside surface of the visor as an effective barrier against condensation in all but the worst condition. But things were cruder and simpler then. It was enough to achieve the basics: helmet on, gloves on, bike started and away successfully. I could finesse the process later and I would learn to do it from experience, not from a book or by listening to someone else. That was the biker way.

★ ★ ★

Finally I'm on my way. Ahead of me is Palace Road, an endless stream of traffic, pressing urgently towards town or out to the cities beyond. I am proud to be pulling on to it on my bike, but a little nervous too. Sitting at the mouth of the side road that runs from behind our house, staring at the rush of traffic is like standing too close to a passing train, waiting on a skateboard for a gap in the carriages. To help with the nerves, I sneer dismissively at the thought of the back-country roads I had ridden in the early days, staying out of town until I had learned to master feeding the power in with the throttle through the clutch and snapping up and down through the gears with my left foot to give my tiny motor a sporting chance of making most use of its power. This is a busy, proper road, not some backwater, bumpkin highway for ferrying spud trucks and cattle trailers to market once a week, and abandoned the rest of the time to lie quiet and undisturbed under a thickening shroud of mud and chewed straw. This feels like the big time. Pulling on to Palace Road on my fifty is like sweeping on to Oxford Street on a Harley.

To my left, at the centre of a big junction a hundred yards up the road, stands a Victorian clock tower, Gothic and heroically gloomy behind a smoke-blackened, grey stone facade that overlooks our front windows. A year earlier I watched from our front room in horrible fascination as a group of bikers on huge, fully dressed BMW tourers, gleaming paint on panniers and fairings, pulled up line abreast at the junction where the clock tower stood. There were seven of them and as they waited to make the turn on to Palace Road they lined up on their smart, top-end riding kit like magnificent, expensive outlaws, spanning the road in defiance of the oncoming traffic swinging off Palace Road past the clock tower. From my vantage point

I leaned forward, rising up on my toes as I craned to watch their thundering departure. But it never came. Instead, the rider at one end of the seven appeared to pick up the wrong foot, lifting his right leg, probably to slot the big tourer into gear, only to realise the lever was on the left; he then lifted his left leg, but without first replacing the other on the ground. A motorcycle won't generally remain upright if unsupported when stationary. This is true and never truer than at that particular moment, as a quarter of a ton of Germany's finest leaned past the point at which the rider's leg could have saved it even if it was in contact with the ground and crashed over sideways. I shut my eyes. Couldn't help it. But my ears saw the damage; I listened as the crash and splinter of plastic fairings and metal cylinder heads hitting the road built and grew more complex, like a seven-track recording as the first bike hit the second, the second the third and, like seven dominoes, they fell. All of them. When I opened my eyes again, the road outside our house was a sea of stranded motorcycles lying on their sides like bomb-blasted horses in a First World War battle. It was genuinely horrible. Gruesome. The confused, bewildered riders threw away all pretence of being cool and wandered among their ruined steeds. I waited for one to pull out a gun and put it to the head of their bike to hasten its sad end. And I didn't laugh.

Today it's my turn to ride past that same junction on a bike, albeit a much, much smaller machine, and I feel that mixture of vulnerability and invincibility that charges up the young biker with righteous indignation long before anything has happened to warrant it. My lip curls inside my crash helmet and I try to move my head smoothly from side to side as I look up and down the road so that passers-by will note the resemblance to a storm trooper surveying a battlefield. The road here is subject to a thirty-mile-an-hour limit, so the speeds are not that great. But moving into an unbroken flow of steel missiles progressing at a little above your potential top speed, each guided by the hands of a driver who hates you for being a biker, is tough. I rev the bike furiously, heart accelerating way faster than the bike will when I finally see a gap and aim for it. The road is slick with rain. Some of the cars still have their lights on, even though the day has now grown as bright as it will get under the steely autumn sky and their headlights leave blurry traces and spider webs streaking across my now badly steamed-up helmet visor. I try to control my breathing, every shaky exhalation making it worse. A break has opened up to my right, further up the road, and if the old fart dawdling in their Metro hangs back just a hundred yards longer I'll have my gap. I get ready to launch, the engine's rasp building, rising and falling as I twist the grip back and forth in my gloved hand. The gap arrives and the revs fall as I let out the clutch and the 2.5 bhp struggles with the bike's inertia.

It's a good pull away. I savour the sensation of walking

that thin line between throwing away the engine's precious power on senselessly spinning the clutch plates and letting the clutch lever out too quickly and bogging it down. A stall is still the worst thing that could possibly happen; a public display of ineptitude that will have my teenage face heating up inside my crash helmet with a childish blush. Not a problem today though. The bike gathers speed and I join the traffic seamlessly.

★ ★ ★

Years later I would experience a similarly heart-in-mouth moment as I lifted off in a helicopter on my first solo flight. Though even that trip would never quite recapture the thrill of pulling off into traffic on my 50cc, aged sixteen. The ride to Ian's house took me through disappointingly suburban pleasantness; smart hedges bordered well-kept houses and neat lanes spurred off the main road to left and right. This wasn't the landscape my young mind and body wanted to surge through on my fiery steed, but it would do. And I was, at least, viewing it from the seat of a moving motorcycle.

Ian was ready to roll when I arrived and by the time I turned the bike in his drive he was fired up and his engine's tinny rasp joined with mine as we climbed the hill out of his lane and back on to the main road. Riding together, two bikes, their engines harmonising and shrieking together, felt impossibly good. We were a gang, a force, we rode through places and they knew we had been there as our rising and falling exhaust notes left their mark on the walls and windows we passed. Sharrow Common was empty when we arrived; we had the place to ourselves and for a glorious hour we rode the course, skinny tyres finding grip where they could in the soft mud. I was cautious, every dip and rise a challenge to be ridden carefully but in the hope of making an impressive spectacle. The patch of scrubland, maybe an acre in total, sat alongside the road, open to anyone, and as we rode it we kept looking across to the tarmac ready to strike an impressive, adventurous pose when any car passed. Afterwards, we sat and smoked as our bikes cooled and we embellished our feats. Ian's drop off a muddy ridge into a puddle became a leap across a chasm, my slip into another, deeper puddle which had ended up with the bike on its side became a huge crash and we would retell it later that night in the Black Bull, if we could get in and get served.

As we sat and filled in the gaps, coloured in the black-and-white frames of our recent experience, a car pulling a trailer drew up in the makeshift car park at the centre of Sharrow Common. The trailer carried a proper off-road bike with angry, knobbly tyres like teeth and a high exhaust under a gaudy plastic shroud. The driver got out of the car and his passenger, a boy younger than us, climbed out and joined him at the trailer. As the man began unstrapping the bike and hefting it down a ramp to the ground the kid – and he really was a kid, maybe twelve years old – strapped himself into proper racing armour: boots, gloves and open-faced dirtbiking crash helmet. Ian and I sniggered and sneered at the idea that this gangly little fool thought he could take on the Common as we had just done. After what had felt like an age, he was ready and his dad helped him up on to the tall dirtbike's skinny seat. We laughed outright at this. The bike fired up with a furious, hollow roar. It was a four-stroke of much bigger capacity than our bikes. It silenced Ian and me. The kid snapped the throttle open and shut a few times, warming the engine before dumping the clutch and tearing into the tracks like a vengeful demon. The dips and crest over which Ian and I had clambered gingerly barely brushed his tyres as he flew across them. He looked like a hybrid between a dirtbiker and a jet-ski rider, the bike skipping across the tops of yumps and bumps as if they were the crests of waves kissing the hull of a speeding craft. His dad looked on approvingly. Ian and I stubbed out our smokes, pulled on our crash helmets and fired up our fifties, their tinny rasps sounding weak and frantic next to the resonant booms from the kid's dirtbike as he threatened to break our precious Common. We rode off. And that was the point. He might have all the kit and a proper dirtbike with a trailer, but his fury was confined to the Common. We took it to the street and were gone.

THE WORLD WAS OUR RACETRACK, 1987

I'm not proud. But I know I'm not alone. I've tried to be honest. You might recognise yourself in here.

The A61 between Harrogate and Ripon was our Silver-stone, our Nurburgring. It was a rally stage, a racetrack and a proving ground. I have no defence because there is none. We were crazy and dangerous and each a potential killer. We operated beyond the limits of our talents and experience and put ourselves in the grey area where only luck and sometimes miracles saved us, and those around us, from disaster every day. Our crimes were not the premeditated exertions of a house burglar or an internet fraudster, they were the joyful explosions of our youthful lust, they were our signature, our shout to the world. We were young. And we were driving. Looking back, I can only say I'm sorry. This passage is not an excuse, nor is it a celebration of what we did, or how we acted; it's an ex-planation of how it felt to do it – or at least it's an attempt to explain.

★ ★ ★

OK, this is it; that roundabout marks the start of it. The A61, the Ripon Road and ... We ... Are ... Off ...

Tricky roundabout, this; there's a bit of negative camber when you hit the middle and a lot of cars are constantly coming in from the Skipton road on the left and the Knaresborough road to the right. But you want to get over it quickly because if you get stuck behind something here at the start you might not get past for ages and then it's all over before you've even started. Nail it, get on to the roundabout before that dreary old goat in the Fiesta joins from the left and ruins the run. And here we go. Whiffs of oil a bit. This car's getting old and that's just the way it smells. Nothing I can do about it. It's got a cool accelerator pedal, the 1976 Toyota Corolla Liftback, just like on a Porsche. It's hinged on the floor and it's kind of long and thin. I think they call it an organ pedal. Like the ones, well, the ones on an organ, I guess. Dunno why it moves such a long way really, I only need one setting: ON.

Short straight now, uphill, bit of a pull, but not a problem. There you go: it's 1600cc this. I know, big and not cheap to insure. Actually my first car was nearly a Capri; looked gorgeous in the picture in *Auto Trader* but my dad went to look at it for me while I was working in the petrol station and it turned out to be stolen. Or at least he thought it might have been, so we walked away. Dad used to work in the law and has a finely tuned nose for that sort of thing. Found this for sale in one of those back-lot garages up the road from Ripon. You don't see many of them around now, mostly rusted away, but this one's perfect. And it's a 1600. I painted the flag on the roof myself. Did it in my cousin's garage. Had to put an electric heater right next to the roof; it was so cold out there the paint wouldn't dry.

Garage selling cars on the right – all way too expensive to even think about. Boring new stuff anyway, for spoiled housewives and blokes who play golf. There's the sign, 'Ripon 10 miles'. Seven and a half minutes, that's the record. I reckon I could do it. Maybe will one day. Petrol station on the left: do you know, I've never been there. Not once. Usually fill at the station opposite home in Ripon. And I do that a lot because I've still got a leak in the petrol tank. Can't risk putting more than a gallon or two in because it drips out overnight. Nowhere to overtake yet, all solid white lines and hatching in the road. Too narrow to risk pushing through, though I'm sure someone will have done, probably Ian's brother. He'd do it. He holds the record, Ian says. Seven and a half minutes from here to the finish at Ripon. But he did some clever stuff to do it; straight-lined the roundabout at Ripley, I'll show you how when we get there. And I think he did it on a bike anyway, not in a car. So it doesn't count. I took a load of us to York in this car once. We were stuck in a traffic jam at the top of a hill and one of the guys threw a lit cigarette out of the window. I suddenly thought about the leaking petrol tank and told them. We all sat there in silence waiting to blow up.

Crest. Right, now you can get past. If you're stuck behind some idiot you can squeeze through here, it's only two lanes but it's wide enough for three cars anyway if you're feeling ballsy. No doubt Ian's brother would do it. But if you do, you've really got to be back in by the solid white lines where the road bends left here, it's not tight but we're on to a bridge now, it's narrow and you'd be in a world of trouble going up the middle here. Wouldn't fit. God that pylon on the left looks cool: really black against the white sky. I'd love to photograph it. Signs saying 40 limit. Still. Why? Road to the left goes to Hampsthwaite. I think I went to a party in a barn there once. Or a village hall. Can't remember. Drunk. Slight right bend now and that garage on the left always has some interesting things in: old Jags and old Mercs, really classy stuff. Some of it's cheap too. God knows what they'd cost to insure though.

Longish pull now and you can get past here – there's a broken white line on my side but already we're into Killinghall and it's down to a 30 limit again. Bollocks. I hate Killinghall. It's only here to slow me down. It's pointless anyway; just a few of those really boring, characterless stone houses. It's all too, I dunno, lifeless. Just a place in a straight line. Not really a place at all. And they're all rich, the people here. How the hell do they get so rich? I stood and looked at a new Jag parked by the road the other day

132

and thought to myself: how can they afford it? And it's not just that. You buy a car like that new – which they will have done, because how could they risk being seen in a car more than three minutes old? – you'll lose more than I've ever seen in my life on it by the time you've driven it off the bloody forecourt. Even if I ever do have that kind of money I will NEVER buy a new car: it's a mug's game.

Sometimes, if I've really caned it to get past someone before Killinghall only to get stuck behind someone else doing thirty, because that's the speed limit here, the person I've overtaken will come up behind me and you can see them being all smug and thinking to themselves, 'Well, what was all that about? I was going at the speed limit and I'm right behind you anyway.' Yes, I know. But they're missing the point. It's not just about getting there quicker, it's about enjoying the journey, the drive. I could probably break Ian's brother's seven-and-a-half-minute record to Ripon, and I wouldn't care if I had to wait outside Ripon until half an hour was up before I could go in. It's just more fun driving fast. It feels good. And if it upsets some people, the people who won't like me anyway because I'm young and have long hair and wear a leather jacket, well maybe that makes it feel even better. I dunno.

Wow, look at that old bloke on the right in the flat cap and dodgy anorak walking the poodle. Now that's a look. What did he do for a living when he was young? Looks

133

like he's ironed his anorak. My granddad used to do that. I'm sure he did. He had my grandmother press his blue anorak so all the creases fell out. I guess he was trying to be smart. Nothing wrong with that, I suppose, if you're old. Truck parked on the right, up on the pavement by the fence, just the cab of an artic; woman on the pavement talking up to the driver. Prossie. Got to be. Probably.

The road keeps sweeping to the right all the way through Killinghall; this bend never seems to give up, but it's gentle and if I weren't in a bloody thirty zone I could give it everything. Christ look, there's another care home on the right. Is everyone round here over a million years old? How many do they need? And that wall there on the right, by the road, with its neat stone cappings and the obelisk and the railings and the little steps; it's all so FANCY. All so twee. And who ever stops here? There's a shop and a petrol station here. Never been to either. Doubt anyone has, if I'm honest. Which I am.

Road bends left and there's the 50 limit sign, which means you can give it everything you've got because they don't really care about this bit. And it's wide enough to get down the middle here. People go crazy when you do it, like you've just sworn at their grandmother or something, but this is a good car, I'm young and in control of it and that dithering idiot has no idea what he's doing. I can fire it straight up the middle and dodge back in again as long as I get back in by the Armco here, because it's on to the bridge next. Doesn't seem to actually go over anything, but anyway it's behind me now. From here on it's all big grass verges and those tall, smart trees like you get in front of stately homes.

I love the way this car changes gear. I love changing gear. Get it right, really snappy, and it feels brilliant. A mate of mine runs a Vauxhall Firenza but he's had it all rally prepared. And I mean properly, not just a spotlights and stickers job; it's got a close-ratio gearbox, sliding Plexiglas windows, Bilstein shocks, the lot. But when he changes gear it's like you've been kicked in the head. I think he does it on purpose, just to make it feel like he's going faster than he really is. I prefer to keep it smooth when I make a fast change; so smooth that your passenger doesn't even know you've changed. They're probably too scared to notice anyway if you're really on it. My dad taught me to brake really smoothly up to junctions, like a chauffeur. You start braking gently, then you can brake harder and then, before you stop, right at the absolute last second, you lift off the brake and let the car roll to a halt. Just about got it now. I'll do it at the next stop. Not that there will be one before Ripon.

Three miles into the run now, trees and fields to either side and we're coming down to the first roundabout in 'the Spanner'. It's called that because there are two roundabouts separated by a short straight, so it's shaped like a spanner. The second one's the most important – I'll show you why when we get there. Not this one though, this one's just straight ahead. I always stay as tight to the roundabout as I can and try and keep it in as straight a line as I can, the way a racing driver takes bends. I love that feeling, it makes you closer to the car, like you're shoulder to shoulder with it, trying to nudge it into the centre of the turn when it wants to leave it. It's intimate and close and violent. Those moments when you get it just right, when you nail it and glide through a bend like it's not even there, it feels like you're carving a line, you could be in a speedboat leaving a long, trailing, curving wake; it takes you somewhere else, somewhere away from ... well, from all of this, all the normal stuff. It makes you feel bigger somehow, like your head has expanded beyond itself and you can see and taste and feel and hear the whole world and everything in it. Connected and remote at the same time, that's kind of it.

This bit between the roundabouts is the handle of the spanner: dead straight and easily wide enough for three cars, so you can get down the middle, between the two lanes. People go spare when you do it. But it's WIDE ENOUGH. It's not like I'm asking them to speed up or anything, they can dawdle along at whatever pace they want on this bit, provided they let me through. If the traffic's really bad here, on a morning or in the evening rush hour, you can dive off at the first roundabout and go through Ripley instead, but it's like a model village through there, all tea rooms and ice-cream shops, and you get the feeling that they're going to go mental and call the police if you do more than thirty so there's no point.

Lay-by on the right, halfway along, truck parked in it. From Holland. There's always millions of trucks from Holland round here, delivering flowers or something. There's a really posh one parks on our road in Ripon, you can hear the coolers buzzing when you walk past it on the way home from a night out. I think they have to keep the flowers cool to keep them fresh. Or maybe warm. I dunno. What do I know about tulips?

You can't straight-line the second roundabout in the Spanner because you have to take the third exit off it and you've got to go further round it in a curve to get there. But here's why it's the most important roundabout in the Spanner: you can do the cheat. If it's really late at night or you're just feeling crazy brave, go round it the other way. Not going to today, too much traffic right now, but I know Ian's brother has done it. Instead of turning left and going all the way round it like this, you go right, the WRONG WAY ROUND IT and fire straight up the exit road to Ripon on the wrong side of the road. I'd probably be as fast as Ian's brother even if I go the normal way round it anyway, just hold it tight to the roundabout then let it run wide through the exit and on to the straight bit afterwards. Like I said, I'm always really careful about my line through bends. Got followed by a police car once. I'd been going too fast, but I think when he saw the lines

I was taking through the bends he knew that I could drive and didn't bother me. It makes all the difference, the line you take. Sometimes I practise my racing lines when I'm walking; I'll try to get close to the apex of the turn by the bottom of the stairs, or keep it wide, ready to plunge in and straight-line two curves together through a door and round an armchair. I don't tell anyone that.

You can go left off there, it takes you through to Pateley Bridge or somewhere, but it gets a bit weird and I thought I was lost when I last took it. Anyway, if you go that way you miss the mile straight further on and the daffodil bends, and you do not want to miss that. Trust me.

We're four miles into the run now; road crests, there's a tight-ish right into a slight left, and then this short straight and now S-bends. God, it's flat here. Gentle right now; it swings left after this crest, though you won't know it when we get there, but you can keep your foot in all the way over and round as long as you then hit the anchors a bit for this next right. I keep it in the centre though, not letting it run too far to the left and then run it out through the turn – there, not too far out, though, because there's an-other left. These bends are amazing. I wonder if different tyres would make it feel different? I guess so. The ones on here are the ones it came with and I hope to God I never get a puncture because there's no way I could afford a new one.

Keep moving through these bends, they're all pretty

much flat out, and five miles into the run there's a real treat. This bend here, blind crest and then the road looks like it's been draped over a lump of earth, like a scarf or something thrown on a bedroom floor, just twisting gently. Sometimes a road can be beautiful, I think. Not because it's surrounded by volcanoes or glaciers or trees full of exotic birds, but because the road itself, the ribboning, writhing tarmac, is beautiful, like a sculpture.

Bollocks. And now we're stuck behind a horsebox. Shit. I don't mind them doing their hobby, that's fine, but why does it have to interfere with mine? This is what I do, I drive, and I love it. And this bloke here with his trailer is ruining it for me. I don't turn up at whatever fields he rides his horse in and rev my engine like an idiot to scare his horse, do I? So why does he have to trail around the place stopping me having my fun? There's nowhere to pass now because we're coming up to Wormald Green. I'll have him on the mile straight, though, if he doesn't turn off first.

My mate Rory lives along here in one of those houses on the left. Once, when Ian had borrowed my bike and disappeared, I was cruising past Rory's house in my dad's car, stuck behind a truck so I was going pretty slowly, and I saw the back end of my bike sticking out of Rory's garage. I turned round further up and came back and stopped here. And when I got to the bike, everything was fine at the back, but the front was totally buggered. He'd crashed it and hidden it at Rory's until he could tell me about it. When I got to talk to Ian again he told me that he'd hit ice just down the road from Rory's house and the bike got away from him. Lucky not to be hurt really, and we straightened the bike out anyway. Said he felt awful about it and I know he did. I'd hate to crash someone else's bike. Haven't got a bike now. Got the car instead. Sometimes wish I had a bike as well as the car, but never instead of it. I've had the car for a couple of months; it's actually for my eighteenth birthday, even though I'm not eighteen yet. But Mum and Dad gave it to me early. I think I might have gone on about it a bit and anyway, they wanted me to have my independence. And now I've got it.

James Whale lives there. That house just along from Rory's. He's a radio presenter and does a bit of TV too. I think I saw him once, one morning after a really noisy party at Rory's. He was leaving the house and getting in his car, a big Merc; probably off to get the Sunday papers or something. Was a great party though; I'd ended up on the roof of Rory's house, trying to get a bottle of whisky out of the guttering. We all went a bit crazy. I was doing pretty well with this girl too, in one of the bedrooms, and I really thought it might all, you know, happen, until a friend of a friend, think his name was Simon, burst in, saw us both half-dressed and everything and burst into tears and ran off. I ran after him to find out what was wrong. He just talked a load of bollocks and I think I might have hit him to shut him up. Or threatened to anyway. Kind of spoiled the moment. Rory used to have some good parties. His parents are pretty cool about it. Hasn't had one for ages though.

Anyway, you can overtake along here, but you've got to be pretty quick because there's a bollard in the middle of the road and the stuff coming down the hill here is not going to be in the mood to deal with you coming the other way on the wrong side of the road. The pub on the corner, on the left, just past James Whale's house, I've never been there. It's just not on our radar and because of that it looks like a picture of a pub to me rather than something I could actually imagine walking into. And thank God, the bloke with the horsebox has swung in. Why's he done that? Who takes a horse to the pub? It's weird, how we have the pubs we visit and the pubs we don't. In Ripon there are something like twenty-eight pubs. I heard it was more pubs per capita than anywhere else in the country. It's only a small market town – well, a city, technically, because it's got the cathedral, but twenty-eight pubs? We have a set route that we travel every Friday night: we start at the Black Bull because it's noisy and everyone's there. My band's played there a few times, Eddie on guitar, Phil singing, me on bass and my brother on drums. We're good actually, really good. The people went crazy when we played the Black Bull. We did our signature song at the end, 'Hoochie Coochie Man' and it lasted about twenty minutes. Folks just went berserk. They loved it. I don't know if people remember that or care when I walk in now. I tend to make myself small when the pub's full and tidy myself away. I'm a small guy and I hate being shoved and pushed about; it feels like everyone's trying to make a point about me being small.

We'll have a Foster's lager in the Bull, or maybe a vodka and lime if we're feeling rich, and then we move on, usually to the Unicorn. It's a really boring pub, one of those bars in a hotel overlooking the Market Place, but somehow it's always good. There's a regular crowd that stay there all night. Then there's a decision to be made. Do we go down to the Water Rat, where it can get really fighty, or maybe the Lamb and Flag, which is kind of an old man's pub but sometimes it gets lively and there's occasionally some interesting people in there. Or we might even walk all the way up to the Spa Hotel and go for a drink in the posh bar there. It's too quiet and fuddy-duddy and I don't know why we go there at all. Except I kind of like it; it feels, I don't know, grown up and a bit safe, like an island in the middle of a night out. It's the place you'd take a date for a meal, I suppose.

So we'll visit another regular pub or two and then make a move either to Gio's or Brontes, the two clubs in Ripon. So far we've been hoping to maybe bump into a girl by accident, or to be spotted by a gorgeous one at the bar who just happens to walk over and say hi because she really fancies you. That's never happened though, so we always end up walking into Gio's or Brontes as just a bunch of lads. There might be three of us in our group, there might be ten, depends what's going on. But it's always just lads. Which club to go to is a tricky one; both are kind of dangerous, if you're me. Gio's is further out of town, towards our house, and it's the cleaner, brighter alternative. There's a big bar and a dance floor and roped-off seating around it. It looks kind of OK, but there's always an undercurrent, something tense underlying it. I feel that tension when I walk into a lot of places, to be honest. Maybe it's only me. Or maybe I can sense it better than everyone else.

The thing is, it's hard to actually meet any girls in Gio's. The place is incredibly loud and always seems to be playing crap like Bon Jovi's 'Living on a Prayer' or, worse still, Europe and 'The Final Countdown'. I hate those fake rock, glitzy glam tracks. I like proper heavy metal: Iron Maiden, Motorhead, that sort of thing. I like rock too; I love AC/DC, even Led Zep. And Deep Purple. But I hate all that big-hairdo posing shit. Although I secretly like Whitesnake. The thing is, the girls like all that shit and if they're going to dance at all, it'll be to Bon bloody Jovi. I don't even know what to do to that stuff. How do you move about to it? I've tried, standing by the roped-off tables, trying to imagine how you dance to it, but I can't. Now, headbanging to a bit of proper heavy metal, looning about with your mates as one big, menacing pack, that

143

I can do all day. And I can pogo around to other stuff. 'Should I Stay or Should I Go?' always has us up and going mental. But the last thing you can risk in Gio's is being seen trying to make a move on a girl. It's too obvious in there – there are no dark corners where you can lurk and talk, nowhere to sort of catch a girl's eye without anyone else seeing you try to strike up a conversation about stuff. That's never happened, to be honest, but I dream that it might every time I go out. Instead, we have to stand around, jammed between the tables and the dance floor, holding our pints of Foster's and sort of sneering, without being busted doing so by anyone else.

I threw caution to the wind one night and just got in there and danced. It was amazing. I must have been drunk and I really got into it, dancing with a couple of girls. It was like a bloody film. It wasn't a busy night, so there were only a few of us dancing, the rest of the lads were sitting and drinking. And then a big bloke, definitely a squaddie, separated himself from his group of equally big mates lounging around a couple of tables at the back and walked up to me on the dance floor. I seriously thought he was coming in for a fight. He looked bloody huge and got really, really close to me. The girls backed off and the bloke put both hands under my chin and lifted my head. I shut my eyes automatically and then opened them, ready for action as he bent down and said, 'I've fallen in love with your pretty little face' and kissed me on the cheek.

His face felt really stubbly and rough against my cheek and his mates just pissed themselves. I'd been puffing my chest out and clenching my fists and I sort of deflated and then felt frozen for a moment. It had clearly been a dare or something. My mates all joined in laughing and so did the girls, and I just did not know where to go, what to say or what to do. I glared at him, hard, hit him with my absolute hardest stare, but he wasn't looking at me any more, he was looking back at his jeering, cheering mates round their table. I turned to my mates by their tables and told them we were off. A couple of them came with me but the rest stayed.

Brontes, now that's a whole different place. It's tucked into a row of shops halfway down the hill to the cathedral. It's beautiful, that little street, feels really medieval, like walking through a Dungeons and Dragons scene. I half expect minstrels to run by with mandolins and lutes, or a maiden being chased by a troll. The door to Brontes is tiny, but inside it's huge. And disgusting. It's absolutely filthy and dark and the paint's peeling off the walls. There are lots of corners and wooden partitions and a dingy dance floor in a corner that always seems to be sticky and full of really nasty blokes and even nastier girls. Last time I was there, I went off to the Gents and saw there were huge clumps of bracket fungus sprouting off the doorframe like elephant's ears. I tried to tell people but they wouldn't listen, or couldn't hear, or they just weren't interested.

145

Whatever. Brontes is probably harder than Gio's; it certainly looks and feels it at first. But where there's a kind of sinister undercurrent in Gio's, it's all obvious and right on the surface in Brontes, much like the bracket fungus. As a result, it's probably much safer. I've not been there many times, to be honest. Some folk are in there all the time, which is probably what makes it so scary. It's too dark, too loud and too full of seriously dodgy people to be my idea of fun. I mean, how the hell are you going to catch some girl's eye when you can't even see her face?

The police wait at the bottom of the hill, outside the cathedral. Some nights, if it all kicks off properly in Brontes, they sit there with the back doors of the vans open, facing up the hill, and wait for trouble to just roll down towards them so they can sort of channel them in, like sheep dogs bringing sheep in through a gate. You've got a big decision to make on those nights out: do you get drunk, assuming you've got the money? Well, you're going to get drunk, that's the point of going out, but do you get drunk early and spend the evening in a crazy, hazy mess, or save yourself and hope to meet a girl and still be sober enough to impress her with your talk? I generally set out to remain serious and sober, but by eight o'clock I've had it, realise I'm never going to meet a girl in Ripon, and get drunk and settle for a half-hearted fight instead.

The thing is, we kind of walk into the room expecting a fight, well, I do anyway, and I'm beginning to think that

146

sort of thing puts girls off. I'd love it if one girl, say a really pretty dark-haired girl with almond eyes and a cruel smile and a leather jacket and silk scarves and biker boots, just saw me in a pub somewhere, maybe by the bar, having a quiet moment and a fag while my mates were fooling about and showing off, and she decided to herself that I was the one, that she preferred me because I'm smaller and quieter than the rest and she could see the potential in me, like something special so she came over, and, well, it all started there. And that has never, ever happened and I'm beginning to think it probably never will. Certainly not in Ripon at any rate.

Right, get to the top of the hill here and it's a tight left, nearly a right angle, in fact. And there it is, that's it: the mile straight. And yes, it is a mile long, because we've all clocked it a million times. There are only two lanes, with a solid white line on this side, which means no overtaking. But the road is wide enough and you can bully your way through if you need to. The verges are huge and wide and soft. I've never actually heard of anyone going off here, but if you did it would be fine, I'm sure. I don't think about crashing, it doesn't occur to me. There's always a way, always a gap, a bit of verge to run on, or the road is slightly wider than you think. It's like, these accidents come along, hungry to get me and then, at the last minute, I manage to step out of the way of them, squeeze past.

Where that massive oak tree is, up there on the right,

that's the crossroads. The road to the left goes to Marking-ton; to the right it goes to Bishop Monkton. Monkton's a big village. It's where we rented a cottage as a family when we were first thinking of moving up here from Birming-ham. Actually, it's where I first met Ian. I was walking around the village with my camera with a massive lens on it, taking shots on a roll of twelve frames of black-and-white Ilford FP4 film that I was planning to process and print myself as soon as I got back to my improvised dark-room at home in Solihull. And I came to a crossroads in the middle of the village; I can't remember exactly what was there, just a few houses and trees and shit. Monkton's quite posh and smart, there's a stream runs through the centre of it with tiny stone bridges going over. Anyway, I saw this guy, about my age, fourteen or so, in a black leather jacket sitting on a wall outside a handsome little building that said 'Mechanic's Institute' in stone letters over the door. As I walked past he said, 'Y'areet?' and I nodded and said 'hi' and we had a bit of a chat about the village and everything and I walked on. I only found out a year or so later that that was Ian, who's now my best mate. And he'd thought to himself, 'Who's this prat with the camera lens like a dustbin hanging round his neck?' And then, when he'd spoken to me and heard my accent, thought I must be gay or Australian or something. But then we met up when I moved to Ripon and joined his school, and became the mates we are now. I'd have loved

The yard was my workshop. Dropping a bolt or a washer in the gravel
was hell.

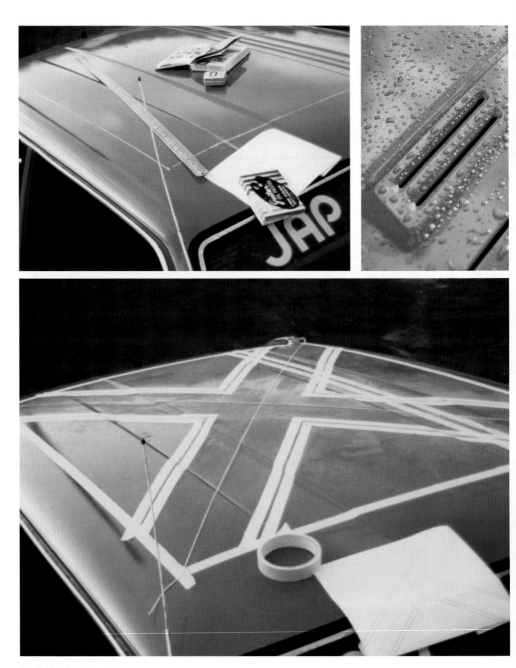

Clockwise from top left

The other half of the windscreen sticker said 'Crap', in case you were wondering.

Bonnet vents. I had vents. I told people about them. These things matter to a teenager. And to a middle-aged man.

Yes, I painted a flag on the roof. What of it?

My eighteenth
birthday. Freedom.

I never made it
to my eighteenth
birthday.

Band practice with our first
band. We played the Black
Bull in Ripon. The folks went
crazy. Apparently. I dunno,
memory plays the nicest tricks
sometimes.

Lead guitarist Eddie. A liability,
but a really talented one.

I still owe Dad twenty-five quid for the scrapyard gearbox but fitting it was one of the best days of my teenage life.

From a distance, you see, it *could* be a WWII Willy Jeep. It's just a case of getting the distance right. Maybe further…

Home. Buttermere in the Lake District. I planted my soul there at the end of my childhood and it's still there. Though probably a bit damp by now.

The walking stick that I found on a barren hillside on Cleveland Way and carried with me across every hill and dale I stomped across since.

A company van was, I had decided by then, a far better thing.

Abbey, my companion on my first grown-up journey. The end of the journey in this book. The start of another…

to get a house in Bishop Monkton and live in the country proper, but we settled for Ripon. Somehow a small town seems even more boring than a small village. Maybe because in a small village people get on and make their own fun, but in a small town they're a bit more wary of each other, kind of more nervous or something. Ian and his mum have moved to Ripon now, anyway, so it all worked out.

★ ★ ★

The road to the left goes to Markington, where I work at the chicken farm at weekends. Have done for years; I started when I was still at school and used to cycle there on my bike at six o'clock every Saturday and Sunday morning. Don't worry, I don't slaughter chickens or anything; it's an egg farm and there are four huts of like, twelve thousand birds in each. Ha, imagine that! Twelve thousand birds in a shed! No, I mean chickens, obviously. It's called 'deep litter', which means the chickens are free to move about inside the shed and then settle in boxes set into dozens of little sheds in rows throughout the hut. It's OK for the birds, they get fed and watered and can move about all they like. As long as they stay indoors. It's probably like a really comfortable PoW camp for chickens, at worst. My job is to collect the eggs: simple as that.

Four of us start in the centre, where the sheds all meet

and there's all the machinery for sending the feed round on conveyor tracks and the water and stuff, and we each take a big trolley, they call it a bogey, that hangs from the ceiling on a rail. It's got a wheel on an arm at the top that hooks into the rail, sort of like a cable car and you can push it around the hut in a big circuit. Each of us sets off into our own hut and you collect the eggs on to yellow plastic trays with egg-shaped dimples in them, thirty-six eggs in each, and then stack another tray on top of that one until you've got a huge tower of them swinging in the bogey. Honestly, you've never seen so many eggs. When we've collected them, we drag the bogeys out to the central bit and grade them and stack them in racks ready for the lorry. Double-yolkers, the really big eggs with two yolks in, go off for baking, I think; the rest are sent off to supermarkets. Or they might go off to be incubated and hatched. I've never paid that much attention because it's not really something I see as a long-term career. It's just a way of earning beer-and-ciggie money.

The noise when you're in there collecting is incredible – twelve thousand chickens all squawking their heads off. It's terrible with a hangover. Worse still is the smell. Twelve thousand chickens all shitting into mud and sawdust. And it's nearly dark too, just low-level red lighting, I don't know why; maybe it keeps them calm or something. Some mornings when you go in at six thirty to do your first collection, the drinking water dispensers have overflowed and the whole place is up to the top of your wellies in shitty mud. The smell and the noise then, as they're all panicking about getting their feet wet or whatever, is just awful. You can almost see it and you can definitely taste it. I threw up once, when I'd spent my entire week's wages on Foster's the night before. All the chickens ran in to eat the carrot and spew in the mud at my feet, and that made me retch again. It's not a job for the faint-hearted. Most of the time the chickens are happy though. Sometimes, in the middle of all the chaos and the noise and the smell, you'll reach into one of the little wooden nest boxes and there's a chicken there, sitting on an egg. They call it 'going broody', when they decide to sit on the eggs to hatch them. That's bad because they then go 'off lay', so we're supposed to watch out for them going broody. But it's so serene, so peaceful, shutting out the noise and smell, reaching your hand into the hut where it's warm and then reaching slowly under the chicken herself, her chest feathers soft on your skin, to feel for the warm, smooth roundness of the egg underneath.

The problem is that often at that exact moment she'll peck your hand, really hard, and it hurts like hell and makes you jump like you've just heard an explosion. I don't blame her, you're trying to steal her baby, I guess, but it's such a horrible shock that after it's happened to you once, you're forever trying to brace yourself for it and you spoil the peace and loveliness of the moment when you first see

151

her in there, all dewy-eyed and content. A couple of times when a chicken's surprised me like that I've knocked the nearly full collecting trays right off the waist-high perch along the front of the nesting boxes, where you put them before transferring them to the bogey, and a hundred or so eggs have smashed on to the floor. Then all the chickens go mental trying to eat them and you're not supposed to let them because then they become 'egg eaters' and go roaming the place like crazy-eyed monsters eating the eggs. Always makes me laugh that, the idea of it: 'Oh no, the "egg eaters" are coming, quick, run!'

Worse though, the cock birds show up when you drop an egg and then it gets really nasty. There'll be maybe a couple of thousand cock birds in each shed; they're in there to keep the chickens in lay, rather than fertilise the eggs. And they're huge. Seriously, these things come up to my waist and are built like tigers. And God they fight. They can take lumps of skin off your arms; they'll sneak up behind you and tear into the backs of your legs as you bend down to collect. One smashed my watch once, with a single peck. They go for anything shiny, so when you've worked there for a bit, like I have, you learn to take off your watch before going in. And you can't scare them off. It's like they don't have whatever it is in your brain that tells you that you can't win a fight. They'll look up at you and then just charge, beak open, right at you. Clout them round the head and they come straight back. If one gets

close, you've no choice but to pick it up, then it'll struggle and peck and kick with those bloody huge talons and
scratch your arms or your face if it can, until you throw
it away. Lob it as far as you like across the shed and the
bastard'll still come roaring back at you, like it's out for
revenge. I'll not lie, I sometimes sort of think I might be a
bit like them. I'd like to be, anyway.

Sometimes it's kind of fun, going into the shed for a
big fight. But sometimes, if you've got a hangover or are
feeling a bit weak, it can get too much. One new guy
turned up once, we told him what to do and he followed
the farmer on his rounds in his shed a couple of times
and then set off for his first solo collection. Only a little
bloke he was, smaller than me even and quite nervous.
Anyway, he'd gone in when we all did and then the rest
of us came out to the main room again and started sort-
ing and packing the eggs on to the big blue plastic racks
ready for shipping. After a while, we realised he hadn't
come out yet. We were nearly through grading and packing; it was practically lunchtime. At this rate the little
bugger might as well just stay in and go round again to
start the afternoon collection. The farm manager went to
see where he was and came out pissing himself laughing.
He'd found him in a corner of the shed, hemmed in by a
million cock birds, all standing and strutting and crowing.
Every now and then one of them would rush in and attack
him. I honestly think they believed they were going to

kill and eat him. And that's definitely what he thought. The manager rescued him and he just took off, never came back. I had to do his afternoon collection on top of my own.

★ ★ ★

Both those roads, the one to Monkton and the one to Markington, are narrow and dead straight at first, which means you're going like hell when you reach the first corner. And there's no room for another car coming the other way; it's too narrow. But you're flat out when you get there and there's no time to think about it, all you can do is hang on through the bumps and jumps and steer round the bends best you can. It's a proper ride and feels like rally driving. It certainly doesn't feel like I'm just driving to work to pick up chickens' eggs for a living.

Those wooden signs at the garden centre place on the left, they've been there for ever. Plants, Fish, Reptiles. Who the hell buys those things? Who needs them? Anyway, they mark the end of the mile straight and it's into a tight right; there's no overtaking now, the road sweeps straight on to a left. I love the trees on the right; they really whip past if you push through these bends. These aren't the best bends, though – those are yet to come. Couple of short straights ahead, between the bends, so you can give it a big squirt, but sometimes the bends catch you – and they're really only the start of it. Because now, eight miles into the run, here they are: the daff bends. Not, as I thought when I first heard them talked about, the 'daft' bends, but daff because of all the daffodils in the verges in spring-time. The verges are fat and round, but nowhere near big enough to accommodate a crashing car. Here goes: there's a crest and a gentle right past the Lodge House – no idea what that is – then out of this right into a left. The road is narrow here, really narrow, there's kind of a hole on the left but you can give a squirt here, pick up some speed again and keep accelerating through this gentle swing to the right, feeling the grip now, tyres rolling across their rims, almost as if the road is breathing in, ready for a left, but it's not, not yet. Stay left and be ready to clip the apex of this right. We're coming up to nine miles into the run now, nearly there. This is tight and at the end of it is a left; it's tighter than you think and it carries on longer than you expect. If I'm going to bin it one day, it'll be here. Set up ready for a right now, lost enough speed, no need for more brakes, push through this right with some throttle going in. Quarry Moor Park is off to the left; I learned to smoke there, but no time for that now. This right is a tight one – well past nine miles now – left, into the 40 limit at the sign, braking as hard as you dare up to the roundabout and there, that's the end of it. That's the run. I haven't set a time today; I wasn't timing it. One day I will, though, and I will break that record.

★ ★ ★

I didn't break the record, but I did bin the car. And it wasn't at daff bends. Waiting to pull out of the junction directly outside our house in Ripon, I made a simple mistake: I trusted an indicator, flashing left on a Volvo estate travelling towards me from the right on the road I was trying to join. I assumed he was going to turn off at the side road before the junction, and pulled out at full throttle with what I thought to be an impressive amount of tyre squeal from the rear. Only he wasn't turning left – the indicator had been left on, probably from when he joined the main road. He carried on and passed in front of me just as I burst out of the junction. I ended up spreading my aged Toyota along the broad flanks of the Volvo like butter on toast. He was a doctor, a responsible adult and a professional at that. He wasn't cross, just calm and business-like as we exchanged details; then he drove off in his slightly dented Volvo and I sat on the tarmac in front of the crumpled ruin of my old Toyota and wept without caring who saw me. My eighteenth birthday was still two weeks away and my present never made it.

DRIVING TO BAND PRACTICE IN A PLASTIC JEEP, 1989

Being in a band was supposed to be an escape,
a fantasy. Fun. And it was, once I'd got there.

From a distance, and I do mean a considerable distance, the Jago Jeep does actually resemble the legendary Second World War Willys Jeep it was designed to mimic. Its compact body has similar proportions, the same flat windscreen, upright grille and simple, round headlights. Ahead of the rear wheels, the body tub swoops majestically down and forward to the base of the windscreen, and it sits high on its wheels, the front ones scantily sheltered under simple, straight-lined mudguards. The problem though, for the owner of a Jago Jeep, is that it is impossible to interact with the vehicle in any meaningful way, say to drive it or polish it, without broaching the critical perimeter beyond which the illusion evaporates. Get close enough to get in and the trick is ruined and the car is revealed for what it is: a cheap plastic pastiche of an historic vehicle whose simple form and undoubted beauty have their origins as much in the car's functionality as in its legendary status and heroic wartime record.

My Jago Jeep had come to me more or less by accident. I had swapped it for a ruined motorcycle. Pleased to be unburdened of responsibility for the bike's inevitable and impending engine rebuild, I had handed over its keys and taken on those of the eccentric Jago with a barely suppressed eagerness that probably worried the guy I was swapping with. This time, I told myself, I had sealed a deal that, for once, would see me avoid financial catastrophe. At last I was in possession of a vehicle I might use to conduct some sort of sensible, useful, functional life.

I was, of course, entirely wrong. The Jeep was fragile, impractical, clumsy, ugly, and inefficient and made me look ridiculous. I loved it. This is the story of how I came to be driving a disintegrating, poorly built plastic replica of a Second World War Willys Jeep over the Pennines on a rainy night in winter 1989 with a gumboil. Hopefully, it explains why this seemingly inconsequential trip in a ramshackle car with a broken bass guitar in the back, an ugly mound of electrical tape wrapped round the base of the gear lever and the remains of a hastily removed sticker on the rear bumper made perfect sense to an eighteen-year-old wannabe radio and pop star. I imagine it will strike a chord with any similarly eager, focused, confused, reluctant youngster trying to force themselves into the world in a fashion that makes the future a more palatable proposition than the dreary mundane lives of the adults around them.

★ ★ ★

As I drove it home that first time, trying to ignore the manky smell and the wayward handling, it soon became obvious that the incredible noise levels were going to be much harder to overlook. The constant rattling of the plastic doors trying to shake themselves loose from their moorings, the grating and grinding coming up from the drivetrain and the impotent mooing of the tired, 2-litre Ford Pinto engine up front all joined in discordant union to remind me of the hopeless truth: my car was shit.

★ ★ ★

Damn it, no, it's not shit. It's a faithful reproduction of the legendary Willys Jeep and I'm driving it because it's a hell of a lot better than the alternative, which is some dreadful, middle-of-the-road piece of crap more suited to taking middle-aged women into town on a shopping spree than to meeting my demands as a keen driver with a sensitive, if rugged, aesthetic. I don't want people thinking I'm some wannabe in a medium-sized hatchback with a set of Halfords' spotlights bolted on the front and a sticker saying 'Turbo' when it hasn't got one. This car is special; it's got something about it. It's got character. It's the choice of an individualist, someone who stands out from the crowd. There aren't many Jago Jeeps out there, and if I ever did see another I think we'd both go crazy, the other driver and I; kindred souls meeting, that kind of

161

thing. I thought I did see one once, in York, but it was a crappy maroon colour and looked kind of wrong, on tiny wheels with pathetic skinny tyres, so I think it was something else. Mine is grey, a really mean, flat grey, like a battleship, and it looks great. The wheels are white with a thin red stripe round them and the tyres are huge.

It's a kit car, the Jago Jeep; you buy the kit, which consists of a massive steel chassis, the body and a load of other bits like bonnet struts and a windscreen, and then you buy a donor car, like a Cortina, for the engine and stuff. You strip the donor car, take out the engine and the rear axle with the differential and the suspension bits, the struts and so on, and then bolt all those bits on to the chassis, bolt the body over the top, fit the seats out of the donor car and there you go: one Jago Jeep. I love the idea of a donor car. It's as though it volunteers for the job. Having got to the end of its natural life, it's happy to donate its engine, its beating heart and its bones for the future of another car. Or maybe it's more like one of those sci-fi novels where the bad guy needs to find innocent good guys and steal their bodies so he can inhabit them and live forever. Something like that.

Anyway, it's running like a dream today. Listen to that: that's two-litres of engine. There's no way could I afford to insure a two-litre in say an Astra or an Escort, even if I wanted to. Excuse the smell, by the way, the carpets get damp when the roof leaks and they've gone a bit mouldy. So, it's a two-litre engine, but because this is a kit car, there are insurers who do special deals on insuring them. I think it's because they realise that, when you've built a car yourself, you're going to take pretty good care of it and are probably the kind of person who knows how to do just that, on the road and in the garage. I do all the maintenance myself. Except the electrics, which are just boring anyway; who wants to spend their time tracing bits of coloured wire back to anonymous little grey boxes with pins sticking out of them?

Feel that? If I hit the throttle hard enough it almost does a wheelie; you can feel the front lift as the back wheels dig in and the weight is thrown back on the soft springs. They're soft so it can go off road. Not that I take it off road; there's nowhere much to go and farmers tend to lose it if you start blasting off across their land. I did take it up to Sharrow Common once. I'd spent all weekend fixing it up, just after I'd changed the gearbox. It had been off duty for a while, probably two weeks stationary with one thing and another, and now it was working again I thought I'd actually take it off road and see what it could do. I drove it up there – the Common's about five miles from home – and took it round the bike tracks. Well, I took it round one of them. Got it kind of hung up on a tree.

I was at the top of a really big slope and didn't like the look of it going down again, so I tried to turn round to go back the other way but the car slipped down a bit and the front bumper ended up stuck against a tree trunk and there was no way I could get it out. It's not actually four-wheel drive, see. The car that the engine came from, the Cortina, was two-wheel drive and so this is too. I guess you'd have to use a real Land Rover as a donor car to make a four-wheel drive version and then you'd just be building another

163

Land Rover, so what's the point of that? Anyway, car hung up on tree, back wheels spinning in the mud, not going to move, so I had to walk home to Mum and Dad's house and ask Dad if I could borrow his car to pull mine out. He went mental. Well no, not mental, he never goes mental, but he did all that 'disappointed in you' stuff. Well, he didn't actually say it, but I could tell he was thinking it when I told him what had happened and why I needed to borrow his car, and he definitely did one of his big sighs when he handed over the keys. I think he thought that because he'd lent me the money for the gearbox, it was an insult for me to then break the car. But I hadn't broken it, just got it stuck. Anyway, he came with me and let me drive his car back up to the Common with a tow-rope, hitched it up, pulled the Jeep off the tree and I drove it home. I was surprised at how easily Dad's Astra Estate made it up to where I'd got stuck. Impressive car, that.

No damage done to the Jeep though; the front bumper is a solid metal box that makes up part of the chassis, so it's bad news for any tree, or anything else it hits. I wish I could see that chassis without the body and everything else on it. I haven't though, because I didn't actually build it. Could have done, no doubt, but I haven't got the tools. Right, watch this, I'm going to overtake that muppet in the Volvo through here. This bit, between the round-abouts at Ripley, is what we all call 'the Spanner'. Here's the critical thing: come off this first roundabout here and look, there's a stretch with space down the middle for overtaking. No good for underpowered cars, because it's too short and you're into the next roundabout. But in this . . . see, it's light and with a two-litre

164

engine it goes like hell. There, look at him. That surprised the shit out of him! Thought this was just another Jeep, didn't he, and then wham, I come flying past at full chat. I don't think he'll make that mistake again.

★ ★ ★

I dreaded the question, 'Did you build it?' People generally asked it when they discovered that my grey Jeep was a kit car and assumed, naturally enough, that I had built it myself. I genuinely believed that I could have done – and maybe I could – and blamed my failure to do so on my lack of tools. In truth, the assembly of such a thing requires little more than a handful of spanners and a hammer. Although even that might have stretched the limited selection of rusty old implements I kept in a dilapidated blue tin toolbox at home. I had assembled my toolkit over years spent rebuilding bicycles and working on my first two cars. But it extended to a few double-ended Halfords ring spanners of an incomplete range of irrelevant sizes pilfered from my dad's shed ten years earlier, an impractically huge and entirely blunt metal rasp, a wood plane that was once my grandfather's, a box spanner of the type used on bicycles but with each hexagonal section rounded off to an almost perfectly smooth bore, a gigantic adjustable plumber's wrench with the legendary trademark 'King Dick' stamped on its huge, rusty flank – God but we laughed at that every time it came out of the box – and an electrical screwdriver with a bulb in the handle that lit if you hit the mains. Armed with this sparse

165

collection I took on whatever tasks my Jeep threw up and tackled them with varying degrees of success. I was making up for not having built it. Our relationship had come to feel like something close to an adoption. Due to circumstances beyond both of our control I wasn't responsible for its creation, but could sure as hell make a good job of looking after it.

The Jeep came to me fully built when I swapped it for the bike. The latter was a Honda CBX750F, the first big bike I'd ever owned, and I had bought it – on finance, before my dismal credit rating made such deals impossible – as soon as I passed my motorcycle test. Having surveyed the offerings within my meagre price bracket in the many dealerships around York, I convinced myself that the CBX750F, with its gawky square headlamps and dated red stripe along its angular flanks, was the best thing I could possibly have. It was the biggest, at any rate, and that was what mattered. It was all about the numbers and 750 was a gratifyingly large one. It also had dash-mounted dials that didn't turn with the handlebars. And that for me was one of the defining characteristics of a truly 'big' bike.

Riding it home to my rented room on the outskirts of York, I had felt incredibly good. This was it, finally, I was a 'real' biker on a machine nobody, not even the most short-sighted of disinterested grannies could mistake for anything other than a proper 'big' motorcycle. Grinning at the noise of the 750cc, inline four-cylinder engine rasping and bellowing through short, stubby silencers, I felt as though my right hand, gripping the throttle in a thin, second-hand motorcycle glove, held all the power in the world. It

166

was empowering beyond anything I had ever experienced to date and, for a while anyway, lifted me out of some of the confusion and frustration of teenage years. On my first few trips out on it, to the shops or to work at BBC Radio York, I felt something that I would later come to realise was akin to the emotion felt by young parents as they parade their new-born in a pram on their first few trips into town, convinced theirs is the most unique and wonderful baby the world has ever seen and that being in its presence elevates them all so far above the ordinary that they float across the pavement. Nobody, I convinced myself, nobody could fail to see and be stirred by the sight of my big silver-and-black bike growling to a halt outside. When my credit card was refused at the cigarette counter in a supermarket in York, I strode in manful silence out to my bike, that I liked to think was lurking menacingly at the kerb, and rode it up on to the patch of grass in front of the store. Holding the front brake on I gunned the engine and let the back wheel spin several kilos of mud up on to the shop window, gradually fading out the surprised face of the till worker inside. They might have been interested to know how terrifying I found the experience, locked in the dark, tight confines of my crash helmet, not really sure if this would work or whether I risked being spat off the bike in front of the store to further deepen the shame of my humiliation at the till.

But the bike had problems. It was old and I couldn't go on ignoring the rattle from the top end that was growing louder every day. I learned that the CBX750F had a reputation for 'top-end trouble'. Failure of the cam-chain adjustment mechanism was common and that could result in the sorts of bills that might in-volve a conversation with a mechanic along the lines of those I have had since in hushed tones with solemn-faced vets across the bowed head of an unhappy dog.

I spotted the Jago Jeep advertised in Auto Trader, my weekly bible. It was hardly going to escape my notice; I devoured every last scrap of the paper each week, dreaming or looking for escape. And sure enough, I discovered that the owner was, as advertised, ready to consider a swap.

I had loved that bike. It had done what I wanted – marked me out as a proper biker. But it had to go. The rattle from the top end was a daily warning that, at some point, the cam chain was going to go and then all hell would be let loose. I was living away from home at the time, renting a room in a little modern house outside of York where I was working freelance at the local Radio Station, BBC Radio York. I rented the room off Andy, another guy at the station who lived in the house too. It wasn't actually his house, he didn't own it; he rented it off the owner. I think she worked at the station too, but she was away somewhere else for a long time, abroad most likely. Andy was further down the line than me, had actually presented a whole show. I was still in the early stages, working as a programme assistant, setting up interviews for the presenters and recording my own interviews to go on air on their shows. The pair of us would sit out in the garage of an evening, smoking and talking about radio and the future. We couldn't talk about bikes; he didn't ride. He'd sit on a workbench or a plastic sled or any of those other things that people always have in their *garage and I'd sit on that bike and we'd talk and drink and smoke. He didn't smoke either, actually. He was tall and good looking and the darling of all the girls at the station and didn't seem to have any bad habits. I used to think of him as being the opposite of me, a version in negative.*

Andy said that one day, soon maybe, the chance would come for me to do the same show he'd done: Last Week in North York-shire. It was the show the station bosses always used to start people on. I couldn't picture myself walking down to the studio with my box of records and taped recordings of all the highlights from the week, or pressing that red button at the centre of the desk to take control of the station and put me live to air. I just couldn't imagine it. Then one day the chance did come. I presented the show. It went well and I did it a load more times. I never stopped being nervous, but the terror slowly left me until I was able to enjoy the job I knew I really wanted to do. That was only on Sundays, and only occasional Sundays at that. The rest of the week I worked as the programme assistant to the mid-morning show, recording interviews and turning them into fun 'packages' for broadcast on the show.

Maybe the big Honda was my way of showing that I might be the little guy on the station, the young lad who goes out in-terviewing farmers about unusual cows or talking to Post Office managers about village life, but I was a rebel at heart and a serious one at that. Didn't always pull it off though. Once, when I came back from the station to the little house on the outskirts of York, I didn't get my foot down properly when I stopped the bike and it went over. I got jammed between it and the back wall of the house. Couldn't get out from under it or lift it off me; it was just too heavy. I had to lie there, wedged under the bike, shouting until Andy came out and helped me lift it up.

★ ★ ★

I don't work at that radio station any more. Got sort of fired because I wouldn't do 'news'. I wanted to be a presenter and that's what I joined to do, to play records and chat and do fun interviews and fun sketches and be there, on the radio, with people through the day. But then the BBC changed everything for local radio and it all became about news and journalists. They got rid of music. I mean, can you imagine it? What's the point of that? If you want just news all day long there's BBC Radio Four, and they've got the money to do it properly. If you suddenly throw out all the music from a tiny local radio station and make the presenters sit there and talk for four hours without a record, nobody's going to listen, are they? I made kind of a fuss. Refused to 'do news', and the station manager, Barry, fired me. Well, he didn't really have to fire me; I never had a proper job to be fired from. He just had to make sure my contract wasn't renewed.

That's why I'm driving the Jeep on the A59 now. I've got some freelance work at BBC Radio Leeds, as programme assistant on the mid-morning show, which is exactly what I used to do at BBC Radio York. I don't live at the house on the outskirts of York any more, there's no need. And I can't afford it, if I'm honest, so I've moved back in with my parents and brothers in Ripon. I'm not going to work right now though; I'm going to band practice. We've got a huge band going now, massive. There are four of us who make up the core: Rob on lead and vocals, me on bass, Chris on drums, Jon on keyboards. Sometimes, for gigs, Rob brings in three girls to sing the chorus, and sometimes even brass players, the lot. Takes hours to set up and by the time we've paid for the petrol and beer we'll be lucky if there's five quid each left in the kitty. But it feels brilliant. You should see some of the bigger gigs, when we've got the full team out. People go crazy. I've seen them dancing on tables, on balconies even. They're only pub and club gigs, but they go on and on and on, and we could, if we wanted, hit the big time I'm sure.

Sometimes, when the wind really gets up or I pick up too much speed in the Jeep, the windscreen wipers set off, blown off their stops, and then get stuck halfway up the windscreen. It's totally flat, the windscreen, just a piece of glass with no curve on it, and perfectly vertical too, so the wipers sit there in the way and the motor isn't strong enough to move them. Once, when I was driving through Middlesbrough to do a day's freelance work at BBC Radio Cleveland, the gear lever came off. I had taken the doors and roof off – you can do that with a Jago Jeep, though it

171

takes a couple of hours to undo all the bolts, and you have to leave the actual roof and doors behind so there's no changing your mind if the weather doesn't play ball. But it's great, driving with the roof and doors off, like you're sitting on the thing rather than inside it.

I was driving through Middlesbrough, roaring and accelerating through the traffic in my Jeep with the roof and doors off and the stereo playing as loud as I could through the old wooden speakers in the back, and when I went to change gear from second to third the whole lever came out of the floor. It had ripped out of the housing. The lever is about a foot and half long and at the far end is the metal arrangement that fixes into the selector mechanism in the gearbox. And this thing flailed up in my hand, so I was holding it up to the sky with the oily mechanical bits at the end looking like it had frayed. I was really embarrassed, to be honest, but I sort of laughed and whooped so people would think it was something I was doing on purpose. Then I pulled over and slotted the selector forks back in so I could change gear. It meant I had to preset the lever before every change, reaching down to slot it back in so the forks on the lever sat over the pinion bit that operates the gears inside the box, which meant it took a long time to drive home to Ripon.

I've fixed it since. Initially I tried taping the gear lever into the box, looping nearly three rolls of that black electrical tape around the base of the gear lever and, as best

I could, underneath the gearbox casting where the lever went in. That didn't work. You can still see a ton of the tape sticking to the bottom of the gear lever. I should take it off, but I've been busy. Anyway, I looked into it a bit more and found that the screw thread in the casting of the gearbox itself had stripped, so I ran a load of that liquid metal goo stuff that comes in a tube around the inside where the thread is and screwed the big nylon locking ring at the base of the lever back in. It lasted all of thirty seconds before it came out again. In the end I had to go to the scrapyard on the outskirts of Ripon and buy a gearbox off an old Cortina. It cost twenty-five quid and I still owe my dad for it. But the best bit was that to take the old one out and put the new one in, I didn't even have to jack the Jeep up; it stands high on its wheels, so I could crawl underneath with the socket set, undo all the bolts on the bell housing, pull the old gearbox off and bolt the new one in.

I absolutely love working underneath cars like that, wriggling about in the dust with spanners. It feels like real work, like I'm a real mechanic. The new one is holding up OK, though it reeks of oil when the engine gets hot. I always work on the car in the bit outside the back of my folks' house in Ripon. It's dusty and the stones dig into your back and it can be really annoying if you drop a bolt or a nut and lose it. I don't talk about that house as being mine any more; it's my parents' house or my folks' house.

Even though I never really moved out of it completely, not even when I was living in the house in York.

We're practising in the basement of a nightclub up on the Skipton road outside of Harrogate tonight. I've got my bass in the back. It's got a massive scar on the front of it where I threw it across the hall in Bedale where we used to practise with our old band. I'd got pissed off with the lead singer and felt I needed to make a big flamboyant gesture. Problem is, the bottom of the guitar, just below where the volume and tone knobs are, snapped off. I glued it back on and where the glue stands up on the red surface of the guitar body it looks like the scar round the neck of Frankenstein's monster, holding his head on. I kind of like it and it doesn't affect the way the guitar works. I've also got my amp with me, though it's on its last legs now. It's enormous, which is why I bought it off a guy in another band, though the fact that it was only ten quid helped. But it's getting pretty tired now and because I always play with it turned full up, the speaker cone is ripped and sounds terrible if I give it even half as much welly as I want to. But there is simply no way I'm going to be able to afford another, so I'll soldier on with it. It looks cool, anyway, even though it's only a combo rather than a proper separate amplifier and cabinet set-up like the pros use. We've got a guy joining us for rehearsal tonight, just to play with us. Rob sorted it and I think he's pretty excited about it. Jason Feddy is his name, and he's a bit of a legend on the blues scene around here. Rob says he's played Wembley, supporting someone really big like Van Morrison or someone. I've listened to his CD and he is bloody good. We'll see how it goes tonight, maybe do a gig with him one day, I'd love that.

Just here, right before you get to Harrogate, where the road gets really broad and goes over a big bridge like a viaduct, I can't go past without thinking of this one particular day at college. Me and two girls, one of whom was sort of becoming my girlfriend, took a day off for the hell of it. I'd never done that before, though I didn't tell them that because they talked of skiving off school as kids; how they used to just take the day off to hang around the shops or whatever. So we three decided one day not to go in to college in Harrogate and to pack a picnic and take the day off instead. I had my old Toyota Corolla then, so I picked them up at their flat and drove to Asda, where we bought sandwiches and crisps and a couple of bottles of cheap wine and then we all travelled out into the country, looking for picnic spots. It was amazing.

★ ★ ★

And it was amazing. The idea came up suddenly in early spring. I hadn't exactly planned on going to art college. Having dribbled to the end of my O-level studies and, miraculously, gained passes in all of them, I had drifted

175

into the sixth form at school with all the drive and commitment of a stick floating along a stream. However, the school and I had very quickly come to an agreement that it might be better if I were to spend my time somewhere, anywhere else. It wasn't that I had set fire to the buildings or stolen the headmaster's car; I wasn't the criminal mastermind type who commits acts of schoolboy naughtiness so atrocious that their legend chimes down the following years full of glory and awe. I was just a pain in the arse, I suspect. I was rebelling with increasing commitment against what I saw as institutionalisation. And I hadn't dealt entirely well with the transition from an all-boys' school to a mixed one. Girls were an object of fascination still and perhaps too intense a distraction for me to concentrate on anything else. Plus my hair was always too long and I was galactically, olympically insolent and smug. And I once climbed across from one balcony to another while the school orchestra rehearsed thousands of feet below me. And when I wasn't fighting boys three times my size or mooning about after girls ten times out of my league, I was lounging around behind the chapel with a cigarette hanging out of my mouth. Basically, by the time my backside had been permanently transformed by the cane into something resembling a hot-cross bun, the school had rather run out of measures by which to bring me into line, short of execution, and a parting of the ways was mutually agreed upon.

Having spent the following summer loafing about trying to be a great artist or a photographer or a writer but with no evidence at all to suggest any of these were likely to become reality in this lifetime, I needed something to do. Art college seemed a reasonable step. There would be girls there, I was sure, and it didn't sound like the sort of place where you had to wear a uniform. The only problem was, there was no proper art college nearby of the sort I had read about in London where real artists were forged in the oils and hog hairs of the studio. But Harrogate College of Art and Technology had the word 'Art' in its title, and the course I enrolled in, Audio-Visual Communications, had at least some vocational relevance, so I figured it might lead me to a job in the media. This was before personal computers had really taken hold, but we spent some time wrestling with early Macintosh machines to produce magazines and used basic PCs to make basic, jerky 3D animations. We painted as well, spending time in life drawing classes trying not to snigger or paint only the rude bits. And we took photographs; I got to use the college darkroom, which made it plain to me just how shoddy my little set-up under the stairs really was. And we talked about art and painters and photographers, people who had really done stuff, big stuff that mattered.

And so, by the following spring we were mid-term in our first year at college studying audio-visual communications and some of our late-teen angst had been briefly washed away by this wave of artistic fervour. We spent our days painting and taking photographs and talking about art and painters, and the whole experience made for a tantalising atmosphere that floated nice North Yorkshire manners and decorum over a layer of fervent lust and deep-seated sexuality that bubbled in our young chests with the same fervour as we were discovering it had under the flouncy shirts and clinging shifts of the artists and models we studied in slide-shows and books. I had been in the process of falling in love with Jane. I fell in love rarely but did so very heavily when it happened. Jane was small and blonde and soft, sometimes quiet but sometimes bawdy and funny and my love for her had developed over the months from a mild curiosity into a familiar, terror-stricken, desperate need, as though she were the only remaining mast on a stricken ship and if I clung to her, focused my energies and thoughts on her and her alone, then I would be safe and all would be well amidst the turmoil around us. The turmoil was around me mostly. She seemed to move around in a state of mild contentment – steady and happy. I hadn't told her how I felt.

Jane lived in a student flat close to campus with her friend Liz, and we three often went to the pub together in Harrogate to talk about music and college, or hung about in college corridors gossiping about course mates and tutors. Liz was more confident than Jane, her short hair was bleached white and her swagger scared some of the other guys on the course. But they made a good pairing; Jane's quiet, artistic sensitivity complemented Liz's confident, ballsy attitude, and I could flit between the two, seeking out solace and indulgence when I needed it or the spark to ignite some necessary piece of teenage lunacy and the confidence to back it up when it was done. I had never had girlfriends before, not in the grown-up sense of 'friends who happen to be girls'. And this was novel and new and terrifyingly soft sometimes. But I was still falling in love with Jane.

We were midway through a lengthy project that required us to create a three-dimensional rendering of a favourite still life using whatever materials we could find to explore perspective and tone. Bored with such a nursery school task, our newly lit artistic flames began licking round the edges of what we felt to be a constrictive and dull box. The weather had been OK for a week now, longer days of soft, constant light through a steady layer of translucent cloud. What we needed, we decided, was a picnic.

I had the car. And that mundane fact soothed and massaged my male ego even within our soft, sexless friendship. I turned up in it outside their flat on a street of once smart town houses in Harrogate at nine the following morning. We drank tea and made plans. Jane loved tea and always made it in a proper teapot with a small degree of oddly touching ceremony. Drinking tea together somehow

179

symbolised and cemented the delicate nature of our mutual friendship. It was sociable, affable and nice.

An Asda store had recently opened close to college and had quickly become the meeting place for everyone on our course and others from across the college. There was a café with bland, corporate seating and a canteen-style counter worked by uniformed staff, and among these symbols of growing Americanisation or homogenisation of our culture we art college students could discuss the important things that we each privately felt made us special and rare in this North Yorkshire town of tea rooms and spa gardens.

We didn't stop for tea or even hot chocolate today but collected a basket of everything we needed. White wine seemed fitting for what was already fixed in our minds as a Georgian picnic. Two bottles of cheapish Chardonnay should do us. I looked longingly at a half-bottle of store-brand whisky but decided it was as inappropriate as it was unaffordable. We discussed food and Jane held out for some Northern delicacy or other, her Whitby accent strengthening as she enjoyed the words and my occasionally mystified face when she stumped me with an especially colloquial reference. She smiled her small, soft smile and her eyes sparkled like a mischievous, impish old lady as she turned theatrically from me to talk with Liz in an accent now too strong and peppered with dialect to be intelligible.

Our picnic assembled, we set off into the morning looking for a site. I had never explored the countryside around Harrogate, it was too close to town to be of any interest and without a car to take them there, Liz and Jane hadn't wandered far either. We drove clear of the outskirts and decided to just carry on driving until we found somewhere we liked, laughing with the freedom of it as we thought of our friends sealed in the studio at college in front of their cardboard models of Van Gogh's chair or Cézanne's skull. This was a wonderful plan, just electing to take a day off, a day out of our lives, to live briefly as other people lived. We wondered why no one had thought of it before.

The right picnic site, we decided, was unlikely to be right next to the road because – and this refrain had grown into a familiar chorus now – 'it's right next to the road'. In a broad lay-by littered with stones and a few beer tins, we drew up a list. It must be by a river and it must have trees, big billowy ones that make a rustling noise in the breeze that was now stirring the bushes alongside the lay-by. And there should be crows too, big fat ones in a lightning-struck tree cawing their hearts out. Liz liked crows and she liked vampire films. *Lost Boys* was recently out and she had seen it several times already and could recite lines and recreate scenes for us as though we were watching it. I hadn't seen it. I still lived at home with my family and Ripon had no cinema. A trip to Harrogate just to see a film was beyond my finances and my nerve. I drove to college every day; I knew the route and the time to be there. But my social life revolved around the Black Bull in Ripon where I sometimes played in a band and from where I could walk home easily, even after spending every penny earned in my weekend work at the chicken farm on watery lager with vodka-and-lime chasers.

I carried the bag. Another shot of chauvinistic habit injected unnoticed into my newly formed female relationships. It was Jane's bag, a brightly coloured nylon gym bag of some sort and a long way from the canvas rucksack I would have chosen for myself or the wicker hamper that the unconsciously agreed theme of the day demanded. I resented the bright blue-and-yellow holdall and hoped that nobody would see me carrying it as we jumped a stile on to a grassy trail between cattle fencing. In the distance we had spied a line of trees, which I insisted marked the line of a river. The girls' ubiquitous Doc Martens were ideal for a yomp in the country, my razor-sharp winkle-picker boots less so and made worse by the jangling chains I had attached as improvised spurs. Liz and Jane swished ahead along the post-and-rail fencing, big boots stomping the last of winter's mud into submission, and they laughed and swung their long skirts. I privately wished for a different jacket; my RAF-blue greatcoat, though fantastically swishable and frocked, was too heavy. I considered taking it off and walking with it draped over my free arm. But it was cumbersome to carry and the black felt waistcoat and contrasting baggy white shirt underneath offered little protection on what was, I now realised, a cool day in early spring. The pocket watch I carried, its chain gleaming across the front of my waistcoat, was for effect more than functionality and I guessed it to be about eleven thirty.

The line of trees did indeed signify a river's solemn passage and I felt a rush of pride as the path took us right to it. The banks were broad and fat and grassy, rising slightly from the fields to the edge of the river where the trees thickened and then thinned along its length. The river was broad here and slow-moving, grey waters swirling lazily and carrying scraps of winter's detritus under a soft, off-white sky. It was the perfect site; even the road bridge upstream to our right didn't spoil it. It was a tantalising reminder of the ordinary dreariness we had left behind for a day.

We had brought a blanket, a small one borrowed from the girls' flat, and it gave us an interesting, unspoken dilemma. To share it would mean uncomfortable closeness, broaching the implicit rules of our relationship. But the ground was damp and cold. We stood and talked about anything other than the sitting arrangements. Jane thought she heard a crow and smiled at Liz and I tried to imagine the three of us intertwined on the multi-coloured blanket now draped lumpily across the long grass at our feet. It was no good; I couldn't picture it without my trousers getting involved. Not acceptable. I shrugged off my greatcoat and spread it on the ground with a flourish and volunteered to sit on that and give the blanket to Liz and Jane. I hid my disappointment as the two perched neatly on the soft blanket, an unwelcome reminder of the disappointments and high stress of being plunged into a mixed senior school for the first time when our family moved North from Solihull. But the sun was beginning to flicker through fast-moving clouds and I hoped for a warm, lazy afternoon by the river.

We talked about art, as best we could. Ours was not a proper art course, it bore an ugly lean towards the vocational, but we could sift through what little we had absorbed about Gauguin and Monet to string together a conversation. And we could talk about films. I lay on my front on top of my greatcoat, chin in hands and listened as Liz, curled up with Jane on their blanket, ran through a few scenes from *Lost Boys* until her feelings for Jason Patric got in the way. We were better fixed to talk about music. Our tastes were diverse but shared a common thread in roots music. Blues and even folk cropped up through the early part of the afternoon. Jane sang a few bars from 'Scarborough Fair' in a voice mellow yet pure and high, and I felt a profound stirring inside. Our few scraps of food had been eaten and the dregs of the second bottle of wine were warming in their green basin and Liz stood up from the blanket. Call of nature. Righto. Bit more complicated for her than for me, obviously. Understood. Jane and I giggled and Liz strode off down the bank in search of seclusion. I lit a cigarette and stretched while Jane moved the light wreckage from lunch into the blue holdall. Without speaking, I moved across to the blanket and lay next to her and we kissed urgently and tightly as I threw the cigarette into the long, damp grass. Liz returned and I stayed resolutely next to Jane on the blanket, an unsuppressible part of me making the statement perhaps that this was my territory now.

★ ★ ★

It's down there, you can almost see where we went from the bridge as we drive over it. We put a blanket on the ground and ate our picnic and drank the wine by the river where the big branches of the still bare trees hung over the river. I've got two brothers, so I'm not really used to just hanging out with girls, if you see what I mean. I've had girlfriends and everything, but that's different. This was just hanging with girls and talking to them, not trying to get after them in a pub or impress them in my band or anything. I've never been so horny in my entire life and was in agony downstairs by the end of the day. Nothing happened, if you see what I mean, but I was kind of deliberately vague about it with the guys at college the next day and let them think what they wanted to think. Which I knew would be absolutely filthy and make me a hero.

There's no clock in this car. The dash is the same grey plastic as the outside, it's all one big moulding, but it's been covered in that awful black vinyl stuff that comes in a roll. The interiors on kit cars are the hardest bits to get right, they never look like a real car, if you know what I mean; something about the carpet stuck to the sides of the door and the way the switches are just standard-issue ones from Maplins or somewhere rather than proper ones made specially for the vehicle by a car company. The lights are a bit shaky too and I'm going to need them soon. It's winter and getting dark. The road on the other side of Harrogate gets really remote, winding up over the Pennines eventually and across the border out of Yorkshire. All the guys who were born round here hate everyone across the border, but I go wherever the radio work is so can't really afford to hate anyone, whichever side of the border they're on.

To be fair, it doesn't drive that well, the Jago Jeep. Actually no, a better way of putting it is that it requires some careful hand-ling and certainly wouldn't be suitable for a really new driver. The engine came out of an old Cortina and yes, it might be a bit wheezy, it might smell quite strongly of old oil when it's worked hard, but it's still a two-litre engine and that's a fair bit of power in a car as light as this. Actually, I once ran it dry of oil, not realising the stuff had been leaking away until the thing heat-seized and stopped completely, bound up tight when the engine got really hot because there was no oil left and the pistons expanded in the bores and became just too big to move. I sat by the side of the road – I think it was the A61 to Harrogate, or one of the back roads that cut through the villages alongside it – and wondered what to do. I couldn't just leave the car, there was no way of locking it and, im-mobile or not, I didn't fancy leaving it there to be stolen or broken into. I'd just fitted those old stereo speakers in the back and wasn't going to let those get nicked.

After half an hour of thinking and smoking, I tried starting it, just for the hell of it. And it fired up and ran fine. I limped it to a petrol station on the Harrogate Road, taking it really, really easy and scraped together the cash for a big can of oil. Sloshed it in and off it went. Fine, like it had never happened. It was like a bloke walking down the street and collapsing with a heart attack and then, when the ambulance arrives, having a drink of water, getting up, saying he was fine and carrying on. Cool. Takes a tough engine to do that. Probably helped that the internals were a bit worn, the pistons not exactly a tight fit in the bores, so soon as they'd cooled off and shrunk a bit, they could move again. It's smoked a bit ever since, probably burning oil where it gets round the piston rings, but it runs and I'm proud of it for doing so.

★ ★ ★

The bond between my adopted charge and me was strong. I felt fiercely protective of it and was quick to leap to its defence in the face of criticism or, more often, puzzlement from those seeing it for the first time. Occasionally that defensiveness would spill over into aggression. Anxious to back up the undeniably strong statement that the car made on my behalf, I emblazoned the rear bumper with a sticker I found at a petrol station: 'Mechanically Inclined, I'll Screw Anything'. I thought it was fun. I was being ironic, of course, but I figured it wouldn't hurt to give people a little jolt when they saw the grey Jeep thundering past. A girlfriend's father didn't see it the same way and it was hastily removed, at his insistence, on the drive of her house. Traces of it still remained, a flash of green and white across the rear bumper.

★ ★ ★

So I strove on towards Skipton in my plastic Jeep. The weather did all the stuff that Pennine weather can. The rain came thick and fast as I crested the hilly ridge out of Harrogate and began the slow wind up to the Pennine range itself. The Jeep's lights, feeble at best, struggled to show me the white lines and when even the lines gave up towards the summit, I navigated by the tell-tale red reflectors on the back of the posts at the side of the road. The noise was incredible. I had fitted a car radio, found or swapped from someone, and connected it to two old wooden stereo speakers from home. I hadn't found a way of mounting the bulky cabinets into the back of the car so they floated free at the end of their elderly wires, shifting across the poorly carpeted load bay behind me when I turned or braked. My bass guitar and bulky amplifier held them in place today though and I could hear them faintly above the rattles and squeaks and roar of wind and road noise.

I hadn't yet learned to embrace and enjoy a hard-charging blast through bad weather in a difficult car; this particular car encapsulated rather too many of my hopes and aspirations as an individualist and someone special, so every failing in it was, I felt, a reminder of my own failings and weaknesses. The wipers were stuck again, jammed halfway up the flat screen where they could do nothing to sweep away the driving Yorkshire rain. Rob and the boys would be waiting for me at the rehearsal. I already had something of a reputation for being late or failing to make band rehearsals. I had explained how my work as a freelance radio programme assistant meant I might be called away at short notice and have no choice but to go. If I didn't do the work, someone else would get it. I missed parties too and weekend lie-ins and careless days in the park playing with frisbees or in the pub having the sort of jolly times and conversations I saw in films.

The boys would be cross if I was late. Well, not cross, but disappointed and that was the thing I wanted to avoid most. I prodded the inside of my mouth with my tongue. I had a gumboil or an abscess by my back teeth. It hurt like hell and poking it with my tongue tasted foul. I ran through the songs we were likely to try tonight: nothing tricky, mostly twelve-bar blues stuff. I was arrogant enough to believe I could play whatever they threw at me and, to a degree, I was right. I was a talented bass player and always looked forward to strutting my stuff. The other three in the band were older and more experienced. The lead guitarist, who was also the singer, had pulled us together from other bands, most of them failing or stagnating, as is usually the way. He was especially good, a serious musician in our eyes, and had the added status of owning the blue transit crew bus we used to transport us, and our kit, to gigs. He was the one whose disapproval I most dreaded. Here was a guy practically there, practically a professional, putting me in a critical role in his band and if I failed to turn up ... well, what did that say about me?

It was no more than twenty-five miles in total to the club where we were practising. But it was rare for me to set off on a journey of any distance with any hope of actually making it in my Jeep. Naturally, I was tense. Driving a car that felt, smelled and sounded like a poorly loaded skip full of builder's refuse falling off a cliff didn't help. That it was supposed to tell everyone how I felt about myself, and my place in the world only intensified that tension. The noise of the plastic doors leaning away from the frames under the pressure of the rushing wind and then slapping back into place as the elasticity of the material was stretched to the limit grew intolerable. It now sounded like a badly trimmed sailing boat being tossed in a tropical storm. I slid the window open, grinding the Perspex sheet across its frame so that the inward rush and tear of wind as it channelled into the car and out through the many gaps and holes in the body took with it the noises signalling impending mechanical failure. It was a constant process of adjustment, changing the set-up of windows, throttle, speed, revs and holding it there until I could bear that particular set of discomforts no longer and boredom and irritation forced me to introduce a different set.

Our first few gigs had been triumphs. We had gelled immediately as a band, perhaps impressed with one another's musicianship and certainly revelling in the chance to jump into a mutually shared repertoire of blues classics and standards and come up with new interpretations in fresh company. Changing bands was much like changing girlfriend, only without the emotional complications. It was fresh and exciting, doing some of the same things but with different people. But that initial flush had lasted only a few weeks. Now we were into the slow grind of trying to find our own, distinctive sound. Looking for the songs that we would one day, doubtless, each import with us into whatever band we next hopped to. Tonight was important because we had borrowed a lead singer. A talented musician, and genuinely so, not in the sense that we attributed talent to many of our fellow operators, touring the local pubs and venues that made up the vibrant and busy but closed and inward-looking music scene of North Yorkshire at the time. We could have found a paying gig every day of the week, but felt it our duty this time round to work hard at getting the band really good before we overworked it. We were, in relationship terms, 'taking our time'.

My gumboil throbbed now and I rolled my jaw as though I could ease the pain like a cramp in a leg. I'd have to get to the dentist. But I didn't know when that might be. I was back at work tomorrow and then there was a chance I might be presenting the Sunday look-back show, *Last Week in North Yorkshire*, the following weekend. Which would play hell with the chicken farm where I worked weekends to bring the pitiful salary of a freelance programme assistant closer to something that might sustain me, and ideally, a car. The drummer had a VW Scirocco. Black and low and lean, I thought it looked the business and was amazed when he showed me how he could drop the back seat and fit his full kit inside it if he needed to. I was quietly envious of his car and could confess to myself, at least, that I wouldn't mind one day stopping this pursuit of a car like my Jeep that impressed the world and settling for something genuine, usable, practical and functional. Something just like Chris's Scirocco, in fact.

The radio had lost its signal and the raw hiss was adding to the cacophony of the plastic car's riotous progress through the bends and sweeps of the Pennines. So I reached down and shut it off. A truck coming the other way had failed to dip his headlights. Incensed with the injustice of it I flashed my own feeble lights at him and signed through the windscreen, mouthing swear words and cursing him to a lonely death trapped in an upside-down burning lorry on the top of the Pennines. The frustration and tension inside me was building daily and everything I did seemed to add to it more than it ever offered an opportunity to release it. The band was supposed to be that release. It could have been. We had no particular ambitions to make it big, we didn't write our own songs or harbour dreams of being spotted. We picked on songs we all knew and loved – straight-up blues tunes, Chicago blues, driving funk numbers, whatever – and worked up our own versions; tight, planned and polished. Sometimes we would work in a section where we'd slacken it off entirely though, or change the tempo, turning a soulful blues song into a skin-tight, funked-up, acid-jazz frenzy. It was heaven for a bass player. Chris was a good drummer and standing alongside him I could enjoy the sort of wordless, telepathic communication that can only really flourish in a hard-working rhythm section of a tight little band. But somehow my teenage need for more, for better or bigger things than anything that was on offer turned even being in a band into something difficult. That was why tonight's journey, which should have been an easy and inconsequential part of an otherwise interesting evening, was so tense in my broken, ridiculous car.

God but my gumboil hurt. Was it a gumboil? Was it an

abscess? I had described it as a gumboil to anyone I'd met, just because I thought gumboil was a funnier word than abscess. Call it an abscess and people might think I was complaining, making a fuss. Worse still, being a wimp. The club was up ahead. I'd been told it was away from other buildings on a corner where the road turned to the left. And it was. An ugly, functional building from what I could see. The car park was exposed to a vicious wind coming in off the Pennines and I opened the rear hatch and dragged out guitar and amp as quickly as I could, the horizontal rain soaking through my shirt and jeans.

★ ★ ★

The practice went well. Jason Feddy was incredible. An affable sort of a guy with a soft, slightly reedy speaking voice bearing a distinct Northern twang, he relaxed and laughed with us. His long wavy hair under a stylish baker-boy cap atop an impossibly loud shirt signalled that here was a guy for whom his music was everything. He was a pro and we were there to learn. We agreed to just try something easy first, an old standard that we'd all know. The film *The Commitments* was only recently out and so 'Mustang Sally' it was. Done. This was weird; it was like a reverse karaoke night. There, in the damp rooms of an empty nightclub, where the carpet and walls oozed stale beer, we as a band were going to play along with a singer whose professionalism meant he could doubtless perform the song as easily and faultlessly as a recording on a karaoke machine. We set up the opening riff, it was familiar to us all but the four of us added our own little distinctive flavour, letting it swing a bit more than we might usually. I couldn't help putting in a little stab on the two and the four from time to time, just to keep it funky. Instinctively, we let the intro run long, setting it up and then running it right through the time-honoured procession of the twelve-bar blues before settling it back into the root and taking it down to let the tension build. No one spoke or shouted commands, no one needed to. We knew this routine and gradually we steamed our way towards the big pause where the singer kicks in with the first line. And when he did, leaning forward, mic gripped in both hands and face hidden behind his wiry locks, so raucous was the sound, so rasping, soulful urgent and good that it truly was all we could do to hold it down and keep it going. It was joyous and we each grinned the special grin that only comes from standing back and listening while you're still right there in the thick of it, playing. I never saw a sign from our own lead singer that this group worship of another voice hurt him. A mark either of his professionalism or generosity, I guess.

At the end of the night, we drifted towards our cars, calling back plans and ideas for an exciting future and agreeing that we must try and get together more often to rehearse. Maybe Jason's voice had reminded us of the gulf between our little band and those who are really good; it was a gulf we were suddenly anxious to close.

I had parked at the furthest corner of the car park, away from the others, and from there I watched as Chris struggled to fit the last of his drums into his Scirocco. He slammed the boot and gave me a wave as he climbed into his sleek, black car, and I waved back, keeping the cigarette in my left hand cupped and hidden from the rain. The others had gone too now and I breathed through the silence, looking down to shield my eyes from the rain and wishing I had a hat like Jason's and the confidence to wear it.

I was standing at the front of the Jeep and could see, spreading from underneath it, the myriad colours and rainbow swirls of oil on water. And this wasn't a fine film, this was a thick slick. Sighing, I leaned forward; resting my right hand on a knee and bending almost double to look underneath my suddenly incontinent car. Oil was still dripping from the back of the sump in the gloom, though obviously a flow that had slowed with exhaustion. I sighed again and brought my cigarette forward to my bent head. And as I raised it and opened my mouth, another substance joined the oil on the tarmac. My gumboil, or more probably abscess, had burst and gleaming strings of blood and saliva hung from my mouth, glinting in the rain and the orange lights from the club's windows. I spat richly and ground my cigarette out into the mess. Ah fuck it, she's run without oil before, she'll do it again. I drove home slowly, dreaming of Wembley Stadium.

RIPON TO BUTTERMERE IN A COMPANY VAN, 1990

A company van was, I had by now decided, a far better thing than a car.

The journey from child to adult is necessarily twisting and sometimes tricky. I had learned that much. And I finished that journey in my favourite place on Earth.

I had tried; God knows I'd tried. But the struggle to stay afloat on a freelance radio presenter's income proved too much. After losing my regular slot as programme assistant to the mid-morning show on BBC Radio York I had drifted into whatever radio work I could find, which meant living in bedsits and on sofas in towns and cities across the North, trying to hold down temporary contracts as reporter, programme assistant or producer. Leeds, Newcastle, Middlesbrough, Carlisle: a new radio station, another bedsit with brown-painted walls in a building haunted by unseen, noisy spectres in the next rooms, and another frightening newsroom full of earnest, committed journalists. I got used to being the new boy, the guy from out of town, the one who didn't really know the patch and who blushed on the few occasions he spoke up in a news meeting with some story he had gleaned from a newspaper and hoped no one else had seen.

Ironically enough, this exposure to different places

would serve me well when I found work producing the *Late Show*, which was syndicated across the Northern local radio stations, but that wouldn't be for three years yet and right now I had to try and gain a foothold on adult life. I was ill-prepared for a nomadic lifestyle. I craved roots, a place, a role; a slot in the world into which I could fit and where I could arrange my thoughts and plans and ideas. I don't think this is unusual at twenty-one: suddenly, all the guidance and help we're offered through our childhood and into our teenage years dries up. We are finished, an adult, ready to go into the world – except we're not. We don't know how to spread our wings yet, but we're too big for the nest.

Society concerns itself with children's education and with containing and nurturing roaming bands of restless, confused and angry teenagers. But a well-brought-up, healthy young man with a handful of O-levels and a temporary BBC ID card doesn't generate the same sympathy and concern. And neither should he. The problem was, I didn't have a clue about how to get on with it. How do you make sure you've got the means to actually get to where the work is? When do you decide your 'relationship' is serious enough to take 'the next step'? When should you think about getting your own, proper place? And how? In each new city, each new radio station, I was surrounded by other young people, probably similarly confused by the push and pull of early adult life, but unable to share it or, perhaps, unaware even of the struggle.

I had to concede; it wasn't working. It wasn't for me. And I had tried to find something that was. Antiques appealed to me, although I knew absolutely nothing about them. The craftsmanship in their creation pulled at my imagination, the sense of history and continuity grounded the anxious charge I had built up in my nomadic travels about the North, and the connoisseurship and knowledge involved in their proper appreciation tickled the snob buried inside me and made me feel a member of an elite club. Plus I got a regular salary and a company van I could use when I wasn't working. It probably all came down to the wheels in the end. I found a job at a local antique pine specialist and I grabbed it and the keys to the van. For the first time in my life, I didn't have to stutter and stumble and explain and re-explain what I did for a living when people asked me. I worked at Pine Finds, simple as that. And if they wanted to know more, I could talk to them about it, as one adult to another. I felt steadied. For a while.

★ ★ ★

Some departures kind of sneak up on you: the moment passes as fleetingly as a shadow and you transition silently from preparation to being underway. At other times it's more of an event. This was of the latter type. The van was loaded. I checked. And checked again, running through my mental kit list: tent – probably wouldn't need it, I would sleep in the van, but good to have anyway – water bottle, compass, maps, boots – didn't plan on anything too demanding, but come on, this was the Lake District. Clothes, stick, stove and cooking kit. I ran my hands over the straps and ropes securing a wooden tea-chest to the bulkhead; it was tied down securely enough for a rough sea voyage. This chest stored the smaller items of kit – I couldn't bear the thought of stuff rattling across the metal floor's ribs for hour after hour and had gone to town with the fixings, using blue plastic rope smuggled out of the cellar and a length of string clothesline of such immeasurable toughness I felt sure it would double as climbing rope in an emergency situation. I would be travelling a hundred miles from Ripon to Buttermere. Basically, get on the A1, head north, turn left and we'd be there. The dog waited by my side in the drizzle, both of us standing in quiet contemplation next to the van at the backyard of our family house in Ripon. This would be a great adventure; I knew that. But it would also be a proper holiday; we would relax.

★ ★ ★

A company van, I was by now convinced, is a far better thing than a private car. Certainly better than any private car within reach of me or any of my friends, colleagues, associates and rural enemies in and around Ripon, North Yorkshire. Look at the evidence: the van was brand new. I had taken over responsibility for it on the day it arrived, fresh from the factory, at the used pine furniture emporium where I worked as salesman, polisher and occasional delivery-man. I had to run it in; probably the first member of the Hammond family charged with running in a brand-new vehicle in generations. My father had never done so to my knowledge, and his father, an ardent enthusiast for all things motoring, had never done so – although he did, briefly drive a Queen Mary tank transporter lorry in the war, before moving into bomb disposal. On the other side, my mother's first car was an ancient Morris Minor called Annabel and her subsequent cars had all been similarly old and variously knackered, so more patching up than running in required. The hottest candidate was my mother's father, who worked in the motor trade for many years. But although he was responsible for seeing hundreds of brand-new Jensen Interceptors off the line and into the hands of waiting superstars of stage, screen and stock market, he had never, as far as I knew, kept hold of one long enough to be called upon to run it in. There was, apparently, a chauffeur in the family on my father's side, I think, but his story was lost in the mists of time and so the field was open to me to break new ground for my clan. These things matter to a young man of twenty. I was going places. I had moved us all ahead and maybe even up by taking over this brand-new van.

It was a handsome van, and sophisticated too. It was a Renault Trafic; about the size of the ubiquitous Ford Transit but lent, I believed, an altogether more interesting and cerebral air by its Gallic roots. Any muppet could pitch up in a trannie full of buckets and hammers, but only someone with that little bit extra about them would roll up the gravel drive to your house in a Renault. And it was a high-top one too, the roofline extended upwards to accommodate the extra volume of the larger pieces of furniture I was called upon to deliver sometimes, having first sold them from one or other floor of the huge, draughty, Napoleonic watermill where the company was based. Sometimes I was sent out to deliver the bigger pieces of furniture with the help of a tall, stringy, dangerous-looking man who smoked endless roll-ups and whose arguments with his wife frequently led to him sleeping in odd places, like ditches and barns, which meant he often smelled funny in the morning. I suspected that he held a particularly vicious dislike of me, but he never showed it in any way I could pin down and explain.

Occasionally, when we had sold an especially enormous Victorian dresser or a triple wardrobe, we would travel in an actual truck rather than my van. It was 7.5 tonnes – the maximum size you could drive on a car licence without an HGV qualification – and it looked to me as big as the houses we would deliver to. I enjoyed my trips out in the truck, even if they were spent alongside a frightening man who I was convinced wouldn't particularly mind if a twenty-foot pine sideboard slipped back down the stairs we were struggling to carry it up and killed me. There's something unnerving about travelling the country with a man who wants to kill you in a truck loaded with large pieces of wooden furniture. The many long pine planks in evidence put me in mind of coffins; those simple rustic ones in westerns where they photograph the dead outlaw, his huge moustache drooping disconsolately, before nailing down the lid and planting him under a pile of rocks on a sandy, sepia-toned hill. I got nervous whenever I saw my sinister colleague with a tape measure.

Trips in the big truck often took us further afield than the more local deliveries I'd make solo in my van; we'd have to make more drop-offs for it to be worth the expense of using the bigger vehicle. And that usually meant an early start. I loved standing by our gate in the very early morning, the sky still coming into focus through white clouds and blue mist and my head swimming with sleep as I waited in the crackling cold for the hiss of air brakes from around the corner to herald the arrival of the truck. The cab would still be misted up, the condensation feathered away delicately at the base of the windscreen by the driver's newspaper lying on the dash. I would haul myself up to the seat, grunting manly greetings to him, this thin sliver of a man whose life away from work took in something murky and earthy and darkly exciting to me. Those were good days, lent an extra edge of excitement by my companion and his rangy ways. But most of all, I loved my solo trips out in my van.

Today though, today my charge would be called into action for something special. Special and, I liked to think, a bit unique. Today my Renault Trafic would be elevated from a proud symbol of my blossoming career in antique pine trading, to become my home. I had planned a holiday, my first ever. I'd been on holiday before, but that was with my parents and they had always planned the trip, bought the provisions, booked the campsite and even, when occasion demanded, organised the foreign money. I had been away on my own too, but those trips had always been under the guise of completing some long-distance walk. Armed with whatever cash I had been able to accumulate as an egg-collector, bookshop sales assistant, potato-picker, gravel-shoveller, petrol station attendant, very occasional radio presenter, painter and photographer and now antique pine furniture salesman and delivery driver, I would set off into the wilds of the Lake District to spend a week plodding over the hills alone, my teenage soul yearning for discovery, revelation, love or poetry and generally finding none. Only the terrible, aching confusion of being a young man in a world that seems to get bigger and more frightening the longer you stare at it.

Those trips then, were not something I ever thought of as holidays. They were adventures. I would hike for thirty miles a day, covering hills and mountains in all weather, sleep a few fretful, lonely hours in a leaky tent before climbing out of a damp sleeping bag and hauling the whole assembly once more on to my back, the thin straps of the overloaded rucksack threatening to cut through my shoulders and down into my chest, and repeat the process until exhausted or I ran out of dried food. The muddier, the wetter, the colder and more painful it got, the better I felt it was for my soul. One rare, sunny day, sitting on top of a craggy hill called Haystacks, I looked past the rocky shoulder of the peak down to the green, flat-bottomed bowl of the Buttermere valley and wept as I watched tiny white flecks of sheep being circled on the broad, flat fields below by black flecks that were sheep dogs, and listened to the farmer's whistles and cries reaching me from the distant valley floor as clearly as if he were standing next to me. As I think I've made clear, I was a fairly tortured young man and on those walking trips, freed from the comforting distractions of daily life, college and work, that torture could intensify nicely to a white-hot, blowtorch flame aimed directly at my confidence, self-esteem, ego and everything else that goes to make up a young man looking for his place in the world. I loved it. At one point, just the sight of a hawthorn bush could move me to mournful tears; something to do with the black, mechanical tracery of twigs

209

supporting white flowers whose delicacy hid a toughness that scared me to the core. Again, I was not an especially happy-go-lucky guy at this time.

This time though, things would be different. This was going to be a holiday. I would take my van with me. Inside, I had set up accommodation, strapping an old armchair to the front bulkhead alongside the wooden tea-chest into which I had stuffed everything essential to a young man holidaying for a week in Buttermere with his Border collie. Her metal food bowl sat on top of the pile of pans and plates and bags of socks crammed into the creaking tea-chest. Alongside the chest, tied to the wire mesh on the bulkhead, was my ancient green tent, there just in case the whole sleeping in the van thing didn't work out. But I knew it would work out. I had no plans to indulge in huge, challenging walks; the armchair was testimony to this. I would slide the big side door open and sit in the chair with my dog at my side, looking out at the hills and the little stream bordering the campsite on Sykes Farm. If I'd smoked a pipe, I would smoke one then. I didn't smoke a pipe and wasn't sure how to go about it. I liked the idea though; it nicely summed up my hopes for a relaxed, thoughtful, rather grown up and gentlemanly holiday.

My aged leather walking boots, brown and glossily thick with wax and dubbin, were tied by their laces to the bulkhead too, alongside my huge and unwieldy walking stick; more of a staff really, a six-foot-long, rod-straight limb I had picked up on a barren and treeless hillside while hiking the Cleveland Way some years earlier. It had lain on the grey shingle and slate, the only organic thing for miles, apart from me and my dog, and I had felt strangely bonded to this once-alive thing. I picked it up, enjoying its heft and swing as I walked with it. I didn't know how it came to be lying there on a harsh hillside not far from the sea, but I trimmed the foot of it with a pocket-knife – an exercise I enjoyed immensely for its manly honesty – and used it for years after. I have it still. It lives by the back door of our house in Herefordshire, more than a quarter of a century after I first found it.

My dog, Abbey, was a Border collie I had taken up with several years ago in the planning stages of an enormous and ambitious walk around the entire coast of the UK. The walk was abandoned for reasons of finance and, if I'm honest, ambition, because I still hoped to turn my part-time radio work into something more full time and felt that spending a year stomping along clifftops and beaches, while stimulating and spiritually rewarding, wouldn't help me along in my media work. But Abbey had stayed with me and would love her holiday in the van. Of this I felt sure. We had gone on many long walks together, often for days on end. We had trekked along the Cleveland Way, the Pennine Way, the Lyke Wake Walk and across count-less hills and dales wherever they lay open and available to our boots and paws. This latest trip, with its new, relaxed attitude towards comfort and exercise, would give us some quality time together, chilling in my van, watching the world go by and each thinking our respective philosophical and canine thoughts. We would doubtless both return from the trip much improved for it. I wonder, do dogs ever smoke pipes? Abbey was with me when I found my walking stick, though she is long gone now. I think of her sometimes when I catch sight of the stick in its rack.

★ ★ ★

Being a delivery driver was not an ambition of mine, I still held on to dreams of working as a radio or TV presenter, even though I had given up sporadic shifts as a freelance reporter at BBC local radio stations across the North in order to take up a full-time job at the Pine Finds emporium in Bishop Monkton. But being on the road as a delivery driver was great, and to be in that romantic, rolling state in a vehicle that stood a chance of actually carrying on rolling rather than threatening to expire at any moment in a cloud of steam and shame was something refreshingly new that I savoured. If the delivery was to Northumberland, I could set off safe and secure in the knowledge that I would, sometime that day, roll into Northumberland. Not something I could ever have guaranteed in any of my own vehicles to date. I was temporarily between cars and, if it were not for my van, would have been reliant on my bicycle or borrowing my dad's car. As an absolute last resort there was the bus. My dislike of using public transport was not on the grounds of snobbery or distaste; I found buses too laden with fleeting moments of encounter and parting, of eyes caught, hopes raised and then dashed at a stop when the object of my feverish imagination and gut-tightening dreams left the bus and floated off without a backwards glance. For a sensitive young man with a tendency to think too much, the bus offered too many opportunities to gaze through rain-soaked windows into houses I would never visit and gardens where people I would never meet played and walked.

But on the road, in my van, I was master and skipper and there were adventures to be had, some of them tragic. I once encountered a pheasant, which I swear underestimated my van, thinking it a lowline, ordinary one. A big, glossy male, he sat in the lane, resolutely refusing to move as my van approached him on the road from Bishop Monkton to Quarry Moor. 'Ah,' I thought to myself, 'playing chicken, are we, Pheasant? Well, let's see what you're made of, my friend.' And, to my subsequent and eternal shame, I didn't lift off the throttle and so continued to bear down on the brave bird. He had obviously worked it out with split-second timing, an impressive feat for a bird that was introduced to this country only for its ability to be scared into flight by men hitting trees with sticks, thence to fly slowly past a line of other men with guns and be shot. But he had based his plans, as was about to be made plain in the most brutal fashion, on the van being of the more humble, lowline variety rather than an altogether more impressive and voluminous highline version such as mine. With admirable nerve, he took off at the last possible moment, giving himself just enough time to clear the top of the van. Or it would have been enough time had the van been lower, which it wasn't. He was, of course, smashed to bits, leaving a lingering sense of guilt in my heart and a nasty dent in the front of my van, right above the windscreen where everyone could see it.

My van had comfortable seats, quite high-backed; sporting, you might say. I did say so, and frequently, to my admiring friends. It had a radio-cassette player on which I would listen to tapes of JJ Cale, Frank Zappa and Howling Wolf copied from my friends' records. These tapes, apart from being illegal copyright infringements of which I am duly ashamed, were trophies. I had acquired them as blank cassettes in the course of a previous job, working behind the till in a petrol station. I would ask customers under my breath if they wanted their collectable tokens and when they didn't hear me ask, keep them and spend them myself on glasses for family Christmas presents and blank tapes to add to my growing collection. I used them once to get a power drill for my dad at Christmas, but such a thing cost so many thousands of tokens I can only imagine I must have stolen some of them and I don't like to talk about it.

I had a clutch of illegally copied tapes ready for the long drive up to the Lake District and looked forward to John Mayall's nasal, tightly played complaints about the unfairness he found in the world, John Lee Hooker's fulsome celebrations of a basic life enjoyed to the maximum and JJ Cale's infinitely soothing, rustic murmur smoothing the miles into a seamless trail.

It had a rev counter too, my van, and I had watched it with incredible concentration as well as burgeoning pride in my thin chest as I set about the process of running in the 1.7-litre diesel engine. Oh yes, 1.7-litres: engines of such capacity were so far beyond the scope of young men like me as to be other worldly, such was the grip that insurance companies held on the ambitions and hopes of young males dreaming of cars and power and all that they might do for our prospects and virility.

Clearly, as the proud first family member responsible for running in a brand-new vehicle, I couldn't call upon my family for advice on the intricacies of doing so. But I had picked up enough information about it over years of sifting through the silt of daily conversations around me for any snippets related to cars and bikes to cope alone. It was all about keeping the revs very low to start with, but not labouring the engine by getting carried away and letting it pull from *too* low down the rev range. This would stress the bearings at the crankshaft end, I think I'd heard someone say. Equally, the engine must not be left running continuously at the same rpm for hour after hour, it's important to vary the speed and gradually introduce higher rpm as you do so. To be frank, I didn't have a clue, but I knew it was very important to treat this brand-new, beating heart with reverence and care and slowly introduce it to the hard labour it would be called upon to carry out for the whole of its life. It felt infinitely special, this business of bringing a new engine into the world. Wherever it went, however many millions of miles it would power this metal carcass around the country and in whoever's hands, I would always be the one who had shaped it, set the benchmark, formed its character. In many ways, I felt I was its creator, its father, and I was determined to be a good one.

The boss's son, Ellis, a thoroughly fun guy who was my occasional opposite number at his father's antique pine emporium, had taken delivery of his van, the same make and model as mine, on the same day as me and had gone about things quite differently. He had set out to abuse the thing from day one as though it were a twenty-quid scrapyard whore rather than a beautiful, newly minted thing to be introduced into the world with all the care and gravitas of a newly fledged eagle. He just got in, slammed the huge door, fired it up and drove it like he'd stolen it. I told him every day that he would ruin the thing, that there was a technique for running in new engines, they had to be eased into service and that the rewards for diligent and careful

216

work at the start would be a better, faster, more reliable vehicle for years to come. Our approaches then, were fundamentally different, and an underlying rivalry crept in.

My van's period of running in finally over, we started looking for opportunities to pitch our two vans against each other, Ellis and I. Such opportunities were scarce. While I was allowed to use my van in my daily commute out to the village from home in Ripon, my route at no point crossed with Ellis's and we were neither of us likely to get up early in order to make a detour on the off chance of encountering one another. But the chance arose naturally on the main road to Harrogate and when it did, it was immediately apparent that his van was measurably faster than mine. It accelerated harder and hit higher top speeds; even its brakes seemed to be better. Mine was definitely smarter and cleaner, apart from the pheasant-shaped dent above the windscreen, but Ellis's was the faster. The woodshop guys found out about our race and my failure and the worst part was they didn't laugh and jeer, they sneered quietly and whistled softly through yellowed teeth and yellowed beards and discounted me forever as a hopeless little fop.

★ ★ ★

But they aren't with me now, those cruel, puppet-faced workers with their confidence in their craft and their

217

menacing beards. We're away on our holiday, my dog and I, and life is going well on board the good ship Renault. The A1 has lain there waiting for us all along as we stood at the back of the house, checking and rechecking our load. Now we finally set sail on it. I love the A1. I love the sense of history being gently buried beneath layer upon layer of honest grime. This stretch of road has been plied for centuries by carriages and horses, highwaymen, charabancs, coaches, holidaymakers, workers, kings and farmers. It's the A1, for God's sake, it must be important. The views to either side through the van's big, broad windows are wide and flat and pale green and brown under a sky of a neutral white that a posh paint company would pay millions to replicate. Stands of trees appear far ahead, growing quickly to black-bristled brushes peeking over hedgerows and then fading to thin black lines of mascara tracing the edges of the hills trailing off behind us.

Next place to pass, Melmerby, coming up on the left. A name I've always disliked. You can't say it without sounding daft. Try it. Clint Eastwood would never say 'Melmerby'; his voicebox would refuse the command and hiss 'Miami' instead.

Junctions flash by, flat interfaces of broad roads travelling to and from places still important, if worn almost flat by the breeze of a hundred years passing over them on this forever important thoroughfare.

Kirklington signed to the left. Sounds ancient.

218

Kirk-lington. Must have had a church there once. Probably still does.

I love the A1. I love its broad, fast bends, the landscape not fully hammered straight and true to conform to mathematics and science; this road is from a time before all that, a time when we were still smaller than the land and we expected to conform a little to its shape as we might step back to let someone pass through the door before us. As if it's only polite to leave in some of the curve and contour, to let the land breathe through the stifling layers of concrete and commerce.

Leeming, that's a nice name. Lee-ming. Sounds gentle. Would make a nice surname. Hold on, I think it is …

Bedale, turn off on the left. Shame to go past, it's a big place, nice town centre. Big square surrounded with loads of those handsome, flat-fronted stone buildings that look like they'd survive a holocaust. It would make a great set for a zombie movie, Bedale. The guitarist in our first band came from Bedale: Eddie. He was a genius, could play a Strat like Hendrix; literally wringing its neck. My brother was the drummer and I played bass. The lead singer was Phil, he could be a bit tricky to handle, but God could he holler the blues and play the blues harp. Sounded like he was a thousand years old and had seen everything. Phil may have been the singer, but Eddie was the band's showman, he couldn't help himself. So we saved up and bought him a wireless antenna for his guitar so he could roam free without a cable tying him to his amp. It was like letting a dragon off the lead. He went mental, tore the place up, balanced on chair backs and ran over tables. The gig was at an RAF officers' club; come to think of it, it was at RAF Leeming; we've just passed it. Eddie crashed about in his big boots on the dinner tables, knocking over glasses and kicking plates and ground his crotch in the faces of the officers' wives as he leaned back and grimaced through a solo that lasted hours. The officers were very angry and we left in our VW transporter without getting paid. Last I heard, Eddie had moved to Germany to turn pro and got into a fight or an accident, smashed all the fingers on his left hand to pieces. Guess his dream ended there. I'd love to know if that was true.

The clouds have thickened, changed from gauze to thick grey sludge, and it's raining those big fat drops that spatter on the van's screen, evenly spaced and round. This will pass quickly; I don't think it will develop into one of those crop-smashing downpours. The noise of the drops on the roof is nice. They hit the broad slope of the van's brow above the windscreen like wet tadpoles bursting. Abbey's asleep and her paws are twitching, anticipating the hills ahead.

North of Bedale and it's here that the A1 loses its 'M' designation and reverts to being simply the 'A1'. I thought this sounded altogether more regal and proper, without the clunky, after-the-event addition of motorway status with its mundane air of civic modernity and efficiency. A coach and horses could travel the mighty A1, manes splaying in the wind and the rush as a hundred hooves smashed and stomped the road into willing and dignified submission. They would never set foot on a motorway, never submit to its hard shoulders and its yellow telephones and blue signs and sliproads and services. The thought moves me and we stand up as we pass Bedale, Abbey leaping to her feet on the seat beside me as I half-crouch at the wheel. She looks up at me with kind, quizzical, hazel eyes as I salute the arrival of the purer A1, unsullied by motorway nonsense. 'Your majesty, your road awaits!' I shout over the thrum and rumble of the van's metal sides. Abbey pants and wags her tail and sits down again, curling into a ball and tucking her nose into her tail. I grin and slot a cigarette between my lips, leaning forward over the wheel to let my forearms rest against it and dropping my head down to bring the cigarette in my mouth closer to the sparking lighter in my hand.

'Well, girl,' I puff the words out through the side of my mouth in a cloud of blue smoke, 'we're on holiday now and nothing in the world can touch us.'

★ ★ ★

JJ Cale crooned to us about the wonders of city girls and their free-spirited ways, John Lee Hooker growled his appreciation of a woman's way of walking about the place and

221

Frank Zappa grew hilariously and rebelliously obscene in his deceptively simple fashion as he sang of a young biker's wager with the devil over a girl's breasts and some beer. We were in high spirits, although the ship was swaying a bit. The Renault Trafic handles reasonably well, for a van. Mine featured the longer wheelbase, which lends it a more relaxed, refined ride on longer journeys. But the high roof makes it vulnerable to crosswinds and it can, when only lightly loaded, develop an alarming sway. We were lightly loaded and Abbey and I looked nervously at one another when the swaying grew more pronounced and we sashayed under grey bridges on the wider stretches. We tried to relax, settled in and listened to JJ Cale's *Grasshopper* album several times through, letting the old maestro's country vibe get us in the mood for kicking back in Buttermere. It's quite noisy though, the Renault Trafic. An effect rendered more pronounced, again, when lightly loaded as we were. The metal sides of the little truck, without bracing from a load of furniture pushed against them, reverberated and shook, transmitting noise from the motorway's grainy surface. Abbey didn't moan or whimper, but I sensed discomfort behind those soulful eyes as she looked up from the passenger seat beside me. I didn't feel too bad for her. The magnificent hills waited for us, solemn in their shrouds of rain and mist. And the public bar of the Bridge Hotel welcomed dogs. And accepted cheques.

Food for both man and dog had been scrounged from

the kitchen of our house in Ripon and stored in the tea-chest with everything else. I loved taking on provisions; it felt like those bits in *Swallows and Amazons* where they talk about stowing tins of pemmican and bottles of ginger beer on their little boat. I loved that as a kid, the idea of taking provisions on board. I didn't have pemmican to load into my van – I don't actually know what it is – but I did have Cup-a-Soups, sliced white bread, tins of tuna, apples and a bag of dried dog food. The rest I was sure I would pick up along the way. Or, funds permitting, I might eat in the bar of the Bridge.

Fuel stop. Ease the joints, let the dog out for a pee on the grass by the car park and face the fact that I needed diesel. In the end, my debit card managing to cough up £10 without protest, though I doubted it would manage the feat too many more times before giving up the ghost and I resolved to go easy on the food when we got there. The burden of young adulthood, with all its neces-sary financial complications and responsibilities, was not lying lightly on my twenty-year-old shoulders. I had re-cently been thrown out of Barclays bank for some minor infringement or other of their rules pertaining to over-drafts and cheques. I didn't really care about my account being closed, but it was the way the bank had done it that wounded. The final blow had been delivered publicly, in the banking hall of their magnificent edifice in Ripon's historic market square, when the clerk had demanded the immediate return of my chequebook and card. His voice echoed off marble walls and he had even held his hand out for the book and the card like an angry commander in a film taking a cop's gun and badge.

People had stared. I had blushed. And I was still cross with myself over how I handled it. I should have swaggered out, playing the rebel, maybe flicked a 'V' sign or told them to go screw themselves. Had I been better informed, I might have made some bold, political objection about the bank's exploitation of people somewhere in the world. Instead, I trickled out on to the street in a dribble of lower-middle-class shame, wondering how the hell people ever climbed out of the mire of gut-twisting, miserable, cheque-bouncing, brokeness in which I imagined I would be condemned to spend the rest of my life. I had opened another account elsewhere and been gifted with a new chequebook and debit card and a new and as yet only slightly plundered overdraft. I may have told a lie or two to open it. I'm not sorry.

The thing about being twenty then, as I'm sure it is now, is that nobody tells you how to do it, nobody explains about how it all works and what you should know to make it work. You're an adult now, so get on with it. But how? I was pretty sure that Ernest Hemingway, Claude Monet and Terry Wogan would have laughed off being thrown out of their bank. But they went on to become Hemingway, Monet and Wogan and that kind of makes everything OK. But it didn't matter right now; I was in an almost brand-new company van, headed for my favourite place in the world with my dog, a new chequebook and the prospect of my first, independently organised, planned and paid-for holiday as an adult lying before me. So things were good. Back on the road then.

★ ★ ★

I love the way the door slams in a van; it's a huge, metallic clang that reverberates around the metal shell. There's nothing soft going on here, no need for sound deadening or vinyl or padding. I slam it, Abbey lies down on her seat. I spark up a cigarette, sigh, flex my eyebrows and settle in for another stretch. Let's go with Frank Zappa again. The tape clatters into the waiting slot. The miles don't exactly fly by, travelling in a panel van, but they do roll and it's a feeling I enjoy. There's a relentlessness to the way a medium-capacity, under-stressed diesel engine burns up those miles one by one by one and plods on. And it does it in a sombre, workmanlike fashion. It's a donkey, not a show jumper, and while it won't wow the crowds, it will get there, whatever it takes. The upright driving position might not look cool, it might not recall the slouching pose of a movie gangster or the prone purposefulness of a racing driver at work, but it's practical and honest and actually very comfortable. And I always feel a sense of camaraderie,

225

looking at the other traffic and watching similar vans bee-tling about on their own business. I've never seen a single, even tiny sign that the same camaraderie is experienced by other van drivers I have encountered. And neither have I signalled such myself. To do so would be to break some sort of manly code known only to the artisans and workers transporting themselves, their products or their ladders, spanners and screwdrivers to work.

Not that I don't enjoy a wave when the occasion de-mands and justifies it. Land Rover drivers do it all the time, though it's complicated. First, you offer a very slight smile, nothing too big or too showy, no need to hurry – there's loads of time to do this, Defenders are bloody slow – and then, if the incredibly subtle smile, no more than the faintest, exploratory up-tilt of the mouth corners is returned, the driver may raise a finger, just the one, off the steering wheel, holding it upright for a second or two while maintaining a grip on the wheel with the remain-ing digits, before returning it into position once the other driver has executed a similar display. On specially signifi-cant occasions, perhaps on a sunny day or, better still, on a snowy day when no other traffic is to be seen and maybe, joy of joys, you have already been able to rescue some lesser mortal in their saloon using your sturdy 4x4, it is ac-ceptable to give a slight nod of the head, more a tilt really, to accompany the finger raise. It's mighty complicated, but boy does it feel good when you get it right. Bikers always nod at one another – unless they're on a Harley, in which case the rider of a Japanese bike must NEVER give even a hint of a nod. And there are other subtleties of behaviour to be observed: if a scooter rider shall encounter a motorcycle coming in the opposite direction it is entirely acceptable for him or her to nod, but they must do so first and displaying appropriate deference to the rider of the larger capacity machine, and they must not register any offence if the nod is not returned. It is the right of the motorcycle rider to decide whether to bestow a nod upon the scooter rider or not. That is their call and theirs alone; should they choose not to nod, it is never appropriate for the scooter rider to look back over their shoulder at the fast-retreating bike and shout 'wanker' or give them the bird. Though it is bloody funny if you do.

Anyway, if I am to gain any sort of acceptance into the ranks of van drivers then I must never, ever give any sign I crave such acceptance, nor that I feel I have earned it. Only then will I be accepted. But, even then, there will be nothing whatsoever to indicate it, no signal or communication or flicker of recognition in the eyes of other drivers. It's probably a lot like being a spy. I know my place among the ranks of bikers and how to conduct myself with intricate precision and social artistry should I encounter a fellow driver of a Land Rover or Morgan – the latter is easy, just go completely mental, not stopping short even of standing up in the driver's seat if you can manage it and throwing your hat in the air (it is a social requirement that you wear one). But take to the road in a van and I am the new kid in school taking his first step into a classroom full of strangers. And these strangers have tattoos, newspapers on the dashboard and fag packets in the door pockets.

★ ★ ★

Back in the van on the A1. Catterick next. And here it comes. Can't see it, just the sign and the road. It's not a big place, but because it's got a huge army base, the town is kind of well known all over. Infantrymen are trained there. You see tanks going to and from it sometimes, hunched on their huge transporters like heavy, green crabs with their claws tucked under their metal shells. God, I love those things. The transporters, that is. Not the tanks. The A1 carries on to Darlington from here but it's joined for a bit by the A66 coming in from the west and running along with it for a mile or two before splitting off to the east.

East and west. I love navigating with a compass. I've got one with me, a Silva compass, that's the flat kind with a clear, acrylic base for aligning it with the map's grid and the compass part is filled with a clear liquid – oil, I think – to damp the needle's swing and make it easier to use when you're walking or running. It's behind me now, tucked into a tired old map case. I hate the map case for two reasons. Firstly, it looks ridiculous, hung round your neck on a piece of red string: I look like a bird spotter. I'd rather give the occasional walker I encounter the impression that I am a wizened old wanderer who knows these hills, but a plastic map case dangling at my waist rather spoils the effect. Secondly, the case is split along one side and lets the rain in. And the rain always gathers at the worst possible place on the map, right on the crease so that when you open it out on your bedroom floor to plan a long-distance walk, you discover that it's rotted through and come apart and you have to sellotape it back together which means you can't trace your route on it with a pen because the pen won't write on the sellotape and you get a gap. And that just looks crap.

We're going west. I love the A66. It's a brooding, sombre stretch of black-and-white road permanently drenched and battered by *Wuthering Heights* weather. The road ahead clings stubbornly to hillsides and makes tight turns at the top of gaping, hungry chasms. It's a serious road, one more suited to business than to pleasure, better fitted to the heavy, plodding trucks delivering essentials to the Lake District than to the countless thousands of holidaymakers and day-trippers fighting for space between them.

The names along the A66 sound old, time-served and proven, but somehow not friendly: Dalton, Forcett, Whorlton, Rokeby, Boldron, Reeth. Turning left here, heading west, it feels as if I am leaving the security and comfort of a county that, while not my birthplace, I can at least call home. I would never presume to lay claim to ownership of any of it, not in the way my friends from school could, with their tales of childhood adventures in a certain patch of woodland, or bicycle crashes on this corner here, under the tree. I was a latecomer to their world; I came here as a fifteen-year-old boy, as fully formed as I would ever be and too late to draw from the land in the making of my character. It was like joining Middle Earth as a middle-aged accountant. But I loved living in North Yorkshire; I loved the hills, the moors we're leaving behind us now to the east, the hawthorns and the walls and collapsed stone barns like broken teeth. I enjoyed the friendly middle-class towns too: Harrogate, where I went to college, with its broad beds full of annual flowers in geometric patterns and its hanging baskets and parks and cobbled streets and unashamed civic pride – pronounced 'praahid'. I saw everyone in Harrogate as a mayor or mayoress, with ruddy cheeks and a thick chain and a suit or dress bought from one of those shops with yellow film in the window to stop things fading in the watery sun. Of course, I was an art student and mortified by the idea of anything quaint, but it made for pretty memories to look back on. Like being raised as a punk in Toytown.

Brough. And my stomach churns here, makes a sideways leap with the thrill of it, because we are getting closer to the Lake District. Abbey sleeps on but I know she is dreaming of the hills, feeling the sparse, rough grass

230

brushing under her paws and blending into the rasp of rocks and loose slate on the barren tops, scoured bare by wind and rain. Despite the prospect of forbidding terrain and harsh weather ahead, the names are softer from here on; rosy-cheeked and big-handed like hill farmers. Appleby, Kirkby Thore, Temple Sowerby: you can hear the accent tighten and twist from a Yorkshire thud to a tight-lipped Cumbrian tunefulness.

And finally, Penrith. From here we will tumble down the A66, turning south-west as we fall into the Lake District in our van. Surveying the voyage ahead in my mind, I see us ricochet like a pinball off the big, brightly lit features of the place, catapulting down towards Windermere's sparkly seaside delights and bouncing back up off Grasmere's soft, fat, thoughtful innocence to shoot straight up Thirlmere's long, sombre banks to the waiting edges of picture-book Derwent Water.

I visualise a map of the whole of the Lake District, the peaks and valleys marked out in yellows and greens and reds. The A66 curves us over the top of this giant's picnic blanket with its creases and folds and we run the very fringe of it, Abbey and me, in our van. On every corner turned I take a dive into the past, every twist, every wall and every stand of trees holds a memory even if only of passing by on some distant childhood trip or college adventure. Troutbeck, the next sign says. I stayed at the youth hostel there as a teenager, three years ago, towards

the end of my coast-to-coast walk. My borrowed rucksack had given up the ghost entirely, the internal metal
frame making a break for freedom through the frayed
stitching at the bottom and leaving the whole sodden assembly hanging down uselessly over my backside, making
it impossible to walk. I slumped into the hostel, finally accepting the fact that the soggy remnants of twisted nylon
at the bottom of my ruined rucksack wouldn't make for a
shelter through yet another rain-lashed night.

At the hostel I met up with a bunch of what older folks
would call 'youths'. That seemed appropriate enough, we
were staying at a 'youth' hostel. We all gathered on the steps
outside like a scene from a play, making up stories about
our respective adventures to impress our fellow youths and
bemoaning the fact that an older couple probably in their
fifties or sixties had pretty much commandeered the com-
munal kitchen to make some sort of middle-aged rubbish
for their supper. 'There's a clue in the title of the place,'
we wanted to tell them. But didn't. I made friends with
a reserved but very funny and artistic storyteller with a
battered trilby hat partially concealing his horribly scarred
face. He told me he had got his scars only a couple of years
back, when his tent had caught fire and melted around
him. I imagined the fiery chaos of it and the pain. We
spoke late into the evening about music and life and swore
to stay in touch. He had no particular agenda to follow and
chose to walk with me the next day. We tackled Greenup

Edge, cheating the start by catching a bus from Troutbeck to Grasmere and laughing and shouting our way through the boggy trudge in the shadow of Ullscarf, neither of us carrying or wearing proper equipment even for this modest adventure, both relying on youth and vigour and the sheer impossibility of getting into difficulty at our age, despite his experiences in a burning tent only a few years back. We parted at Stonethwaite, from where I carried on to Buttermere and he disappeared back to Scotland, I think. We never did stay in touch. People seldom do, really.

The road from Troutbeck spills down to Ullswater, where we holidayed as a family a thousand years ago and I stayed in a youth hostel for the very first time. We sat by the water through an evening so long and warm and sunny that there was room in it for another entire life. But we pass the sign for Troutbeck today and head on to Keswick. It's just a town, there are shops and buildings, some pretty, some not; it's full of people shopping and spending all the money I haven't got on all the equipment I want but will never have. I've never enjoyed Keswick, with its crisp-edged houses and neat front gardens and pavements worn thin by a million hikers avoiding any hiking in favour of shopping and tea rooms – it's got a 'pencil museum', for God's sake! But it's a gateway, the entrance, and from here it all gets better by the mile. Passing through the Lakeland town, I look at Abbey and wonder if we should stop; this is

233

the last town we will travel through before we get to Buttermere and I shan't be leaving the valley's embrace until our week there is over. But stop for what? I don't want to shop, I feel above it. I don't need the latest rucksack or a jacket made of a technical fabric that lets your skin breathe. And I sense my newly minted debit card breathe a sigh of relief, ironically enough, at the conclusion. We swing south on the B5289, the Borrowdale road, and we are now travelling the final corridor leading us to heaven.

Running along Derwent Water's edge, the narrow road dips down almost to the lake in places and I feel a tiny jolt of excitement when it does so, as though earthing a spark of static electricity from a fingertip against the water. The road makes a million small rises and turns, twisting to follow an ancient route conforming to fields and rocks and trees that have never been commanded to lie down or move for us. I push the van as hard as I dare. I should slow down, take it in, relax; I'm on holiday. But I am excited and full of a young man's energy and driving as hard as I can is my celebration of this place, my way of being as alive as the trees and ferns and the earth they stand in. Pale white dapples of light splash over us as we pass under trees whose branches touch tips over the road. The drystone walls run right to the edge of the road, crowding in on corners so that we sway round them blindly, heart racing in anticipation of the turn or drop we will meet on the other side. With the van as lightly loaded as it is, the thing leans and rolls and I can feel the solid, leaden weight of the engine up front counterbalancing the heaving sides, doing all it can to keep us from tipping. If a car were to appear round this next bend ahead, we would crash head-on; there would be no alternative. And someone would be hurt, maybe me or maybe an innocent family on holiday or a farm worker dashing into Keswick for supplies. And it would be my fault, the fault of the stupid, hormonal charge of energy and excitement flooding through me and flushing out sense and kindness ahead of it as it drenches my cells.

Faster. The noise, the thrill, the pace of it, it's a song to the sky, I'm releasing this energy that otherwise would make me explode. I'm hauling on the wheel, almost standing to heave at it as the van rolls and lurches, bracing myself with my knees and steering with my whole body, my stomach muscles and shoulders fighting to balance and turn. The diesel engine moos and moans like an ill-tempered cow being prodded up the ramp into an abattoir truck as it is brutalised and provoked within its narrow rev range. It's not built for this, not made to be pushed and revved and braked and pushed again. This is a brutal act, a desperate thing, close to a fight, but I am smiling, grinning, laughing, I feel alive at these times when I could so very easily be dead. And this last bend here, just at a crest in the road where the way swings left only I can't see further because it passes around a steep rock taller than the van's high roof and as close to the road as if this were suddenly a tunnel. Hard on the brakes, I steer left, hauling on the big wheel and I feel the weight tip forward and right, hurling its dumb energy at the front tyre which squirms and protests, but it grips. I'm grimacing now, keeping it tight to the inside of the turn but anticipating the rock's sharp bite into the flimsy sides of the van as we pass round. It doesn't bite and there is nothing coming the other way and we are all alive and I slump into the seat, driving slowly now, taking deep, shaky breaths and whistling them out through pursed lips. 'You OK, girl?' I breathe. Abbey looks up, she's braced on the seat's broad cloth, her legs must have worked hard to keep her from plunging down into the footwell. 'Nearly there. Nearly there.' I smooth my hair back. It's still long, almost down to my elbows, and I reach behind my head to gather it up, gripping it tightly in a sweating palm and pulling it back behind my shoulders.

'Anyway, girl,' I relax my shoulders and stretch my back, 'we're on holiday!' I half-yell the proclamation and reach for my cigarettes, grinning again. This pack had better last at least until tomorrow.

Leaving Derwent Water where it fumbles to a raggedy stop in broad, lush meadows under thick, dark grasses, we head out on the final stretch. Here we pass into a landscape from a fantasy novel, Hobbity and ancient. Rosthwaite, Borrowdale, Seatoller; tiny villages, hamlets really, with a few houses on a bend in the road and a post office selling postcards or a hopeful restaurant, waiting like a spider to tempt tired walkers. Rosthwaite, Borrowdale, Seatoller, I tick them off. These names are burned into my memory, scoured there as surely as water and wind eat away the Lakeland granite to leave their marks where they choose. I can dream my way through them and do. I have walked through these places, passed by them on some lonely slog, hauling my home stuffed into a borrowed rucksack and leaning on my stick to ease blistered feet in soaking boots. It's gentle down here, among these little villages from a storybook and with the drama of a hilltop passage at Scafell Pike or Great Gable behind you. Before you know it, the weariness creeps in and your thoughts turn to food and beer and talking. Today though, we're drifting through, serene and cosy in our van, the storm at the lake has passed and I know all that waits ahead now is my favourite place on earth. Swinging around Seatoller, we begin the climb up to Honister Pass.

Climbing: it's what I come here to do, to ascend these hills and fells. And with every metre gained, there's a feeling of getting closer to something pure and essential. It's a simple enough thing, walking up a hill; it's easy on the mind, it's rhythmic and plodding, but it's also tough and draining. And to my twenty-year-old imagination, if it's tough, it must be good. It's not a fast activity, nor a heroic or impressive one; there's no thought for what people will

237

think, whether anyone will be impressed, whether I can boast about it afterwards. No, I'm just slogging my way up this big hill so that when I get there, I can admire the view or strain to see anything through the rain and the clouds and then walk back down the other side, maybe to repeat the process on the next summit and the next until collapsing into the limp, damp, enveloping embrace of a sagging tent by a stream at the end of the day after heating humble food in a single pan over a tiny stove, my whole being suffused with that indefinable air of weariness, exaltation and righteousness. I don't seek out the big-name, glamorous summits, the glossy ones that people collect with the same gravitas and meaning as they might collect vouchers at a supermarket. In fact I avoid them. I've climbed them all, but their well-worn paths offer no more chance of meaningful escape than motorways or rail tunnels. I seek out the simpler hills, the lesser ones, the ones whose summits don't quite make the grade in metres on maps but whose peace, solitude and romantic splendour sing to me.

Climbing is good then, even if the climb is made at the wheel of a company van. And I am climbing now, winding my way up to the Honister Pass and sure enough, for every metre gained, I feel the same gentle flush of light-headed righteousness as if I were making the climb on foot. Maybe more so, because I know that this climb is taking me closer to Buttermere and the start of my holiday. For one stretch here, it's an incredibly steep climb too. I have

238

walked it, of course. My brother, Nick, was with me and we were making our way up to the pass at the top and our best route took us, briefly, along the road, but after only a few short, sharp miles we would swing left and set out over the stark, slate-studded slopes to approach Fleetwith Pike and on to Haystacks before walking the ridge around Buttermere, passing High Crag, Sheepbone Buttress, High Stile and Red Pike and Bleaberry Tarn before dropping down to the lake itself, clambering down Scale Force and the beautifully named Sour Milk Ghyll. I savour the names, running through them in my head like poetry or spells.

The scene broadens, the hills stretching and rolling, straining against their ridges and edges. Under the thinning drape of pale, rough grass, slates glint and twinkle in the white light as we climb. Just rocks now. The sky is lowering towards us like a watercolour, the road ahead twists and turns, threads a way around solitary giants; single stones left standing after wind and rain have eroded the ground around them. As the landscape widens, the road narrows and dwindles to a fine black ribbon ahead, taking me up towards the Honister Pass. And I reach it, the pass, this cramped and narrow groove through the ridge separating Borrowdale and Buttermere. Men were here before Wordsworth and Wainwright; maybe even in Roman times they came to plunder the mountain of its glinting black treasure, carving and hacking to stir the intoxicating mix of industry and wild nature that inspired the poet and the wanderer.

There's a tipping point at the top, a final turn, a final crest and there is the Buttermere valley. My mind snap-shots, time-slices the last instant as we cross and it's as though I can stand, frozen in time, balanced on tiptoe with arms outstretched like a diver on the highest board and breathe in, drawing power from the great chasm in front and below. I'm ready to fly down there now, to swoop and curve off the slate walls and granular hills before coming to rest in the velvet cup of the valley. In an instantaneous blur I consider everything that worries me, every nag-ging concern; maybe I'll get the chance to work back at the radio station, maybe it will turn into something more, something bigger, maybe I'll succeed, maybe one day I'll understand what success is and maybe my new bank ac-count will hold out. A wife, children, a home of my own, respect, ambition – all of these things and more I gather up and tuck under a rock, just one of millions up here at the pass, before I begin the long, lazy swoop down to the valley.

'We're home, girl,' I tell Abbey. 'Home.'